Early Rome and the Etruscans

Robert Maxwell Ogilvie was educated at Rugby and Balliol College, Oxford. He was a fellow of Balliol from 1957 to 1970 and headmaster of Tonbridge from 1970 to 1975. He is now Professor of Humanity at St Andrews University. He has written several books and articles on Roman history, religion and archaeology. He is a Fellow of the British Academy.

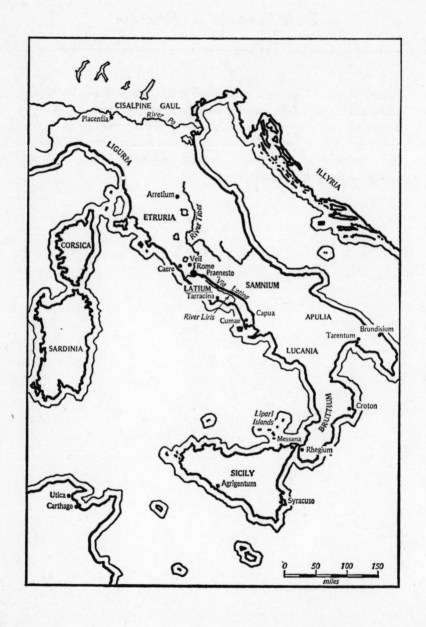

CISALPINE GAUL
Placentia
River Po
LIGURIA
ILLYRIA
Arretium
ETRURIA
River Tiber
CORSICA
Caere
Veii
Rome
Praeneste
SAMNIUM
LATIUM
Via Latina
Tarracina
River Liris
Cumae
Capua
APULIA
Tarentum
Brundisium
SARDINIA
LUCANIA
Lipari
Islands
BRUTTIUM
Croton
Messana
Rhegium
SICILY
Agrigentum
Utica
Carthage
Syracuse

0   50   100   150
miles

R. M. Ogilvie

EARLY ROME
AND THE
ETRUSCANS

THE HARVESTER PRESS
By agreement with Fontana

THE HARVESTER PRESS LIMITED
Publisher : John Spiers
2 Stanford Terrace,
Hassocks, Sussex

Early Rome and the Etruscans
This edition first published in 1976 by
The Harvester Press Limited
by agreement with Fontana Books
Fontana History of the Ancient world, Volume 1

ISBN 0 85527 086 1

Printed in Great Britain by
Redwood Burn Limited
Trowbridge, Wiltshire

Contents

Illustrations

Introduction to the Fontana History of the Ancient World

No justification is needed for a new history of the ancient world; modern scholarship and new discoveries have changed our picture in important ways, and it is time for the results to be made available to the general reader. But the Fontana History of the Ancient World attempts not only to present an up-to-date account. In the study of the distant past, the chief difficulties are the comparative lack of evidence and the special problems of interpreting it; this in turn makes it both possible and desirable for the more important evidence to be presented to the reader and discussed, so that he may see for himself the methods used in reconstructing the past, and judge for himself their success.

The series aims, therefore, to give an outline account of each period that it deals with and, at the same time, to present as much as possible of the evidence for that account. Selected documents with discussions of them are integrated into the narrative, and often form the basis of it; when interpretations are controversial the arguments are presented to the reader. In addition, each volume has a general survey of the types of evidence available for each period and ends with detailed suggestions for further reading. The series will, it is hoped, equip the reader to follow up his own interests and enthusiasms, having gained some understanding of the limits within which the historian must work.

Oswyn Murray
Fellow and Tutor in Ancient History,
Balliol College, Oxford
General Editor

Introduction

Over the last twenty-five years the study of early Roman history
has moved at great pace. In part this has been the result of the
exciting archaeological discoveries made in Latium and Etruria since
the war, particularly at Lavinium, Veii and Pyrgi: in part it is due
to the acute analysis of the historical sources associated with the
names of such scholars as Momigliano, Alföldi, R. Bloch, Werner,
Toynbee and Palmer. The interaction of archaeology and history has
inspired far-reaching reappraisals of the whole character of early
Rome. It may, therefore, seem superfluous to add one more account,
but I think that the time has now come when a more detached, less
speculative and more robust history can be written on the foundations
which others have laid. I have deliberately started with the sixth
century because it is then that the history, as opposed to the pre-
history, of Rome begins, and I have tried to set out the evidence,
and the criteria on which that evidence must be evaluated if history
is to be written. Even so the field is often controversial.

One particular point requires preliminary explanation. The
problems of the chronology of the early Republic are at present
insuperable. It is probable that the temple of Jupiter Optimus
Maximus was dedicated in 507 BC and Rome captured by the Gauls
in 386 BC; but a conventional system was devised, perhaps by the
scholar Varro in the first century BC, which dated these two events
in years which correspond to 510 BC and 390 BC respectively.
This system has survived in most history books to the present day.
In absolute terms, therefore, most of the events in fifth-century
Rome are likely to be three or four years out: for example, the
Battle of Cremera is traditionally placed in 479 BC but is likely to
have been fought in 476 or 475 BC Given the overall uncertainty,
however, and the danger of confusion which would result if one were
to revise all the traditional dates, I have retained the Varronian
chronology. I also considered but rejected as too unwieldy the
technique used by Toynbee who gives three dates for every event

(e.g. 471 [or 468 or 467] BC). In the last chapter, dealing with the capture of Rome, I have distinguished the traditional dates from the true dates, because Roman affairs are, for the first time, interlocked with a wider international scene.

Finally I should like to thank John Pinsent who has discussed these matters with me over many years and who subjected the original draft to a most searching and constructive criticism.

ERRACHD

Traditionally Rome was founded in 753 BC but even in antiquity there had been many variant dates proposed, ranging from 814 to 729 BC. Apart from some short-lived Chalcolithic and Bronze-Age settlements the first substantial habitation at Rome dates from the Iron Age. Unfortunately, the archaeologists still disagree radically about its date; some would put it as early as the tenth century whereas others favour a date around 800 BC. What is clear, however, is that there were two separate and distinct settlements, one on the Palatine Hill and one on the Esquiline, almost from the beginning. The burial customs and the pottery styles of the two settlements are quite different. It seems probable that the site of Rome, with easily defended hills, at a convenient crossing of the river Tiber and with good pasture, attracted two separate groups of graziers from the Alban and the Sabine mountains down to the lusher coastal plains.

Early Rome was primarily a pastoral community. Its inhabitants built their huts on the tops of the hills and during the daytime led out their flocks and herds into the surrounding country. The ground-plans of some of these early huts (one of which, the *casa Romuli*, was preserved as a museum piece down to the Empire) have been recovered and we can form an idea of what they looked like from urns, made in the shape of huts, in which the ashes of the dead were stored (Plate 1). The earliest inhabitants were a branch of the Italian people, an Indo-European tribe that had spread over Italy during the second half of the second millenium BC.

The advance of Rome, however, was due to the expansion of her mysterious neighbours to the north, the Etruscans. Some time, perhaps in the tenth century, groups of migrants, probably from the Balkans, arrived by sea in North Italy. Some of them came up the Adriatic and settled in the Po Valley (e.g. at Spina and Bologna), others came round the bottom of Italy and settled on the west coast at Tarquinii

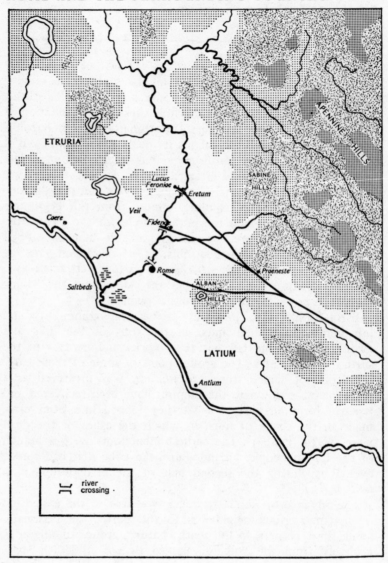

ETRURIA

APENNINE HILLS

Lucus
Feronike
Eretum

SABINE
HILLS

Veii

Caere

Fidenae

Rome

Praeneste

ALBAN
HILLS

Saltbeds

LATIUM

Antium

⊐⊏ river
crossing ·

and other places. Both groups share a distinctive custom of
burying their dead in two-storeyed urns which is obviously
related to the great Urnfield cultures of Romania that flourished from about 1600 BC. In Italy this culture, which absorbed the native population, is called Villanovan. The Villanovans were reinforced around 700 BC by a new wave of
immigrants, probably displaced from Asia Minor by the
troubled conditions of the Cimmerian invasions. The new
arrivals brought with them many fertile ideas, including a
taste for Greek and Phoenician artistic styles, new techniques
for working metals, an aptitude for building proper cities
rather than untidy villages, Near Eastern religious customs
and, it seems, a sophisticated non-Indo-European language,
preserved in numerous inscriptions but not yet fully understood, which we call Etruscan. This mixture of elements
transformed the Villanovans into the Etruscans, from a simple,
agricultural people into an urban nation of craftsmen and
traders, with a network of cities that stretched from the Po
to the Tiber.

The Etruscans were enterprising and outward-looking. They
sought markets for their metal-work (there are large deposits
of iron and copper in Etruria and on Elba) and for their
pottery, and in return imported luxury goods from Greece,
Egypt and Phoenicia. It was, therefore, inevitable that they
should open a land-route to the Greek cities of Campania
and Southern Italy. The easiest routes lay a few miles up-
stream from Rome where there are good crossings of the
Tiber at Fidenae (near Veii) and Lucus Feroniae. The road
then led southwards past Praeneste, between the Apennines
and the Alban Hills, to join the line of the Via Latina and
on to Campania. But the site of Rome had other attractions.
It was the last point before the sea where the Tiber could
conveniently be crossed and so it gave access for the Etruscans
to the rich plains of Latium. More important, salt was
essential to the life of the great Etruscan cities inland and
it could only be obtained at the big saltbeds at the mouth of
the Tiber. Some time towards the end of the seventh century Etruscans from South Etruria began to infiltrate the hut-
community at Rome.

From this point onwards Rome is largely an Etruscan

city, a fusion of native and Etruscan elements. But – and
this is perhaps as important – the history of Rome was not
one of steady progress. In the period covered by this book
I hope to show that Rome's fortunes fluctuated, with a high
point under the last kings and a low point – so low indeed
that Rome might have vanished for ever – in the closing
conflict with the Gauls in the early fourth century.

2 Sources

The reconstruction of early Roman history is made exceedingly difficult by the nature of the material. On the one hand there is relatively little archaeological material. Some of the nearby towns such as Caere, Veii and Lavinium have been fairly thoroughly explored, but because Rome has been continuously inhabited for 2,500 years, excavation can only be conducted in random places. The Roman Forum provides the largest single area, but even here the discoveries have tended to be piece-meal and controversial. Nowhere can one get an uninterrupted and continuous picture of the evolution of the city. Nor is there much contemporary evidence in the way of inscriptions recording laws, treaties and the like. Only about a dozen inscriptions of any historical value, whether in Latin, Etruscan or Phoenician, survive from before 400 BC and most of these are fragmentary and obscure. We know, from ancient sources, the contents of perhaps as many more which have not survived. Some of these, such as the Twelve Tables (p. 120) or the Latin Treaty (p. 100), are of the utmost value for the light which they throw on political and social institutions.

On the other hand the literary sources have to be handled with circumspection. There are several elaborate accounts of the period. In Greek the writers Diodorus Siculus (writing about 40 BC) and Dionysius of Halicarnassus (7 BC) give detailed versions of the early history of Rome, while in Latin the historian Livy (began writing about 29-25 BC) devoted five books to the period from the foundation of Rome to its capture by the Gauls in the early fourth century, and the statesman Cicero (died 43 BC) in a number of his oratorical and political works, notably the fragmentary On the Republic, a discussion of the ideal state against the background of Roman history, dealt at length with episodes from the remote and glorious past. And there are countless anecdotes and allusions in other writers. The questions, however, that have to be asked are: How reliable was the material that *they* used? Where did *they* get it from?

There were passing references to Rome in some early Greek historians, but the first account of any length was not composed until the beginning of the third century BC when a Greek, Timaeus of Tauromenium, took an interest in her affairs. The first Roman to write his country's history, Q. Fabius Pictor, did so at the end of the same century – and wrote in Greek, the only available literary language at the time, with a view to establishing Rome in the eyes of the world as a civilized and great nation, at a time when she was fighting for her life against Hannibal. It was political and patriotic history. A generation later, the elder Cato compiled the first history of Rome in Latin – a work called *Origins* which concerned itself with the foundation-legends and early doings of Rome and other Italian cities as well as with more recent times. We do not know the scale of Timaeus' work, but it is significant that Cato certainly passed from the period of the kings straight to relatively modern events, and Fabius Pictor must similarly have treated the early Republic extremely scantily. A newly discovered inscription gives a summary of his work which confirms the impression already known from the fragments preserved in other authors, that he was primarily interested in the legendary past:

[Quin]tus Fabius, surnamed Pi[cto]rinus, a Roman, so of Gaius.
He enquired into the arrival of Hercules in Italy and (?) the alliance of Aeneas and Latinus . . . Not (?) much later Romulus and Remus were born . .

The foundation and regal period could be supplied with a wealth of imaginative detail, transplanted and adapted from Greek mythology and history, but not so the early Republic. The inference to be drawn from the structure of Cato's and Pictor's work is that they had very little material at all for the fifth century. One can think of possible records – copies of treaties, dedications, laws; family archives; funeral monuments; lists of magistrates and officials – but they would have required patient research to yield any coherent historical framework. And there is a further stumbling-block. Much

of the material that might have been accessible to Cato or
Pictor, had they wished to use it, had been destroyed in
about 390 BC. As Livy says, commenting on his own difficulties:
'In that period [before 390 BC] writing, which alone is a trust-
worthy guardian of the record of past events, was but rarely
used and even what was recorded in the commentaries of
the pontifices and in other private and public memorials
perished when Rome was burnt.' (6.1.2)

Nevertheless, by the time that Livy and Dionysius of Halicarnassus are writing, the pages are fat with apparently well-
documented events. The magistrates of each year are named;
minor wars and battles are solemnly chronicled; trials are
described; political manoeuvrings are followed through in
painstaking detail. Where has all the information come from?
Is it fact or fiction? Livy spoke of the 'commentaries of the
pontifices' as a major source and we know something about
them. Cicero (*On the Orator* 2.52) writes: 'The chief pontiff
used to put in writing the events of each year and publish
them on a white board at his House (the Regia), so that the
people could take notice of them'. The same thing is said
four centuries later by Servius, the Vergilian scholar (on
Aeneid 1.373): 'Every year the chief pontiff had a whitened
board, headed by the names of the consuls and other magistrates, on which he used to note day by day memorable
events, at home and at war, by land and sea'. Some idea of
the contents of his board are conveyed by Cato's scornful
remark that he did not wish to record the kind of events
that figure on the pontiff's board – 'How often corn is dear,
how often the sun or the moon is eclipsed.' Or by a typical
passage of Livy dealing with the events of the year 295 BC
(10.31.1-9):

The Samnites made raids on the land of Vescia and Formiae.
The praetor Ap. Claudius campaigned against them. In
Etruria, Q. Fabius, the consul, killed 4,500 citizens of Perugia
and captured 1,740 who were ransomed at 310 asses each.
All the rest of the spoil was distributed to the soldiers. This
year, so successful in war, was filled with distress at home,
by plague, and with anxiety, by prodigies: for accounts
were received that in many places showers of earth had

fallen and that many soldiers in Claudius' army were struck by lightning. Carefully the Sibylline books were consulted. Q. Fabius Gurges, the consul's son, prosecuted some matrons on the charge of adultery. They were condemned and from the fines he built the temple of Venus near the Circus.

All of this is the raw material of real history, and Servius goes on to say that it was published in eighty volumes and known as the Annales Maximi. The date of publication is not precisely certain, but was during the pontificate of P. Mucius Scaevola, consul in 133 BC. One might assume, therefore, that subsequent historians were able to write in detail about the early years of the Republic in a way which Cato and Pictor could not. And certainly historians do refer to the pontifical chronicle for events in regal and early Republican Rome. It is the authority claimed for the fact that Numa was a pupil of Pythagoras; Cicero, who says that the Annales recorded events from the beginning of Roman history, quotes them for an eclipse of the sun on the Nones of June in the 350th year of the city, to be identified with an actual eclipse that occurred on 21 June 400 BC. But can these Annales have been authentic? Livy, after all, says that they had been burned. It is inconceivable that the notice about Numa could be genuine. And how would they have been preserved in any case? The Regia is too small to have stored several hundred large boards. The contents must have been copied down onto a roll, presumably for the purpose of providing the pontifex maximus with a handbook of religious precedents for dealing with unexpected situations.

It is a matter of great dispute. On the whole, my own conviction is that the Annales did largely survive. Livy indeed says that one of the first tasks of the pontiffs after the fire of 390 BC was to recover and reconstruct their records. There is too much that is of major significance which can be verified archaeologically such as the dedication of temples, or the inroads of the Volscians, for one to reject the records utterly. And too much of complete insignificance, not worth anybody's time, whether in the fourth or the second century, to invent. Names of obscure places and even more obscure people have the ring of truth about them. Moreover, Rome is unique among ancient peoples, except the Chinese, for the care with which it preserves the memory of ancient institutions. Roman society and its institutions were very traditional. Whatever historians might care to invent about the character and doings of individuals, there was a clear and unchanging tradition about social institutions which a modern scholar can very largely rely on. The relationship between the client and his patron, the duties of religious priests such as augurs or pontiffs, the ceremonials associated with great festivals, the crucial legal procedures which defended the rights of the free citizen (*provocatio, perduellio, vindiciae,* etc.: see pp. 127 ff.), all of these rose out of certain historical and social conditions which can be reconstructed in consequence. The Romans were proud of that side of their conservatism – the tradition of their forefathers (*mos maiorum*) – and it forms the bed-rock on which we can build up what we know of them.

Nevertheless, great caution is needed. The Annales, if they were based on original material for the period before 390 BC, were certainly written up in a romantic and fictitious way. And equally certainly they were incomplete as the chronological gaps and dislocations reveal. It is, moreover, surprising how rarely they are quoted. Cicero did not suggest that here was the obvious reference-work when he wanted the names of ten legates who had served in Greece in 146 BC. And Livy makes no effort to consult them at first hand. Perhaps there was only one, inaccessible, copy. But if they are in any way reliable, they provide the only material for an objective history. There was indeed other evidence – family records, oral tradition, inscriptions – but it is supplementary to the annual chronicle which the Annales afforded. Nevertheless, as Momigliano has emphasized, Roman aristocrats, unlike their Greek counterparts, were deeply interested in what their ancestors two centuries before had, or might have, done and there was a long tradition at Rome of personal memoirs.

Cato and Pictor, therefore, dealt with beginnings, by compiling legends and assembling folk-memories. A new generation acquired some actual facts on which to construct a detailed and coherent history. Their work does not survive, although we know that it was extensively quarried by Livy and Dionysius of Halicarnassus for their own creations, and we can gain some idea of the techniques which this middle generation of historians, men such as Valerius Antias or Licinius Macer who were writing between 80 and 60 BC, used to expand and elaborate those facts. It was universally accepted by the Romans as a literary (or psychological) technique that people act in character and that, therefore, you could assert things of people for which there was no actual evidence but which would have been characteristic of them to have done. Sp. Cassius (see p. 110) was said to have been a demagogue: very little is known of him, but, because he was a demagogue, he will have acted as historical demagogues, such as the Gracchi, did. So a historian was entitled to transfer the measures and policies of the Gracchi and attribute them to Sp. Cassius in order to give his life more verisimilitude. A few Fabii attempted to withstand the whole might of Veii, as the Spartans had done against the Persians at Thermopylae. So it was legitimate to take over many of the details of Thermopylae and retell them in the context of Cremera.

This kind of type-casting affected the history of the kings even more, because there was less hard evidence for their characters and their achievements. It had become fashionable to think of history as something of a cyclical process which moved from the good (Romulus and Numa) through intervening stages to the bad (Tarquinius Superbus) and in which each king had a clearly defined role. Romulus was the warrior-founder, Numa the priest-legislator (so that all religious innovations are attributed to him), Tarquinius the Elder the city-builder, Servius Tullius the founder of the constitution, Tarquinius Superbus the tyrant. Facts and stories are fitted into this preconceived framework.

The flesh and bones of early Roman history as established by these middle-generation historians were taken over by Diodorus, Livy, Dionysius and others – and it is their work which survives and which we have to use in order to reconstruct how the history has been built up. Diodorus wrote a Universal History in which early Rome did not figure extensively, but Livy and Dionysius treated it spaciously. However, they were interested not so much in the political aspects as the artistic and moral. They were concerned to create literary works of art and to this end it was legitimate to mould, embellish or suppress elements of the traditional story as artistic exigencies demanded. The events had also to express the personalities of the leading historical figures. Here again there was licence for adaptation and imagination.

Dionysius and Livy were contemporaries. Dionysius, a Greek, was born in Halicarnassus on the coast of Asia Minor, which was also the birthplace of Herodotus. We do not know his exact date of birth but he came to Rome in 30 BC, at the close of the Civil Wars, a mature man with an established reputation, as a teacher of the art of speaking and writing (rhetoric). So he must have been born about 60 BC. At Rome he devoted himself to the study of Roman history and after twenty-two years of research published in Greek his *Antiquities*, as his history of early Rome is known. Of this large work eleven books survive together with scanty fragments of another nine. The surviving portion carries the story down to the middle of the fifth century.

Dionysius was a modest and reticent man, who tells us nothing of himself as a person. We can only discover a little about him from his literary contacts. In addition to his history he wrote letters on literary criticism which he dedicated to individuals. Some of the recipients are fellow scholars, who are virtually unknown (for instance Ammaeus and Pompeius Geminus) but others were public men of note at Rome, such as Q. Aelius Tubero, a member of a distinguished literary and public family, the father of the consul of 11 BC, and Metilius Rufus. This mixture of men of letters and men of affairs was characteristic of Roman society in the period 150 BC – AD 150 and it gave Dionysius the *entrée* to a group that had the material and traditions without which a history of Rome could not be written. In that respect he resembles another of his contemporaries, whom he mentions, Caecilius of Calacte, a Jew from Sicily, who also made his mark at Rome as a rhetorician and a writer.

Dionysius' work is characterized by three special qualities. The first is the detailed research that went into it. Dionysius, unlike Livy, read voraciously, especially the earlier historians

who, writing in Greek, had touched on Italian affairs – Phere-
cydes and Antiochus of Syracuse (fifth century BC) and
Timaeus and Q. Fabius Pictor (third century). Again, unlike
Livy, he had investigated at first hand the Roman antiquarians
– men like Cato, Tuditanus and Varro, who collected the
oddities of the Roman past whatever their bearing on actual
history might be. He was lucky to be in Rome at a time
when public and private libraries were without equal, and
he clearly used them to the full. For example, he is one of
the very few writers of antiquity who knew and availed
himself of the Third Book of Aristotle's *Rhetoric*, 'On Style',
which had been brought to Rome as part of a large and
famous library by Sulla fifty years earlier. He also immersed
himself in highly specialized discussions of the pre-Roman
inhabitants of Italy with a wealth of detail and argument
that baffles elucidation. Who were the Aborigines? Who were
the Oenotrians and the Arcadians?

He was, therefore, an extremely well-read and careful
scholar, by the limitations of his age. But he was also a
Greek, and a Greek of Asia Minor, and there was something in
that background that coloured a writer's historical approach.
All the East Greek historians, from Herodotus downwards,
were fascinated by the origins and foundations of cities,
and such enquiries took up a quite disproportionate amount
of their works. So it is with Dionysius. The first two books
are full of abstruse and intricate discussions designed to
establish the parentage of Rome, not because Dionysius was
chauvinistic and wanted to prove that all that was best at
Rome was really Greek in origin but because it was a subject
of burning interest to him and one on which, for a very
cautious man, he was prepared to offer original solutions.

But the third characteristic of the work is its extremely
formal structure. In one of his works of criticism, *On Imita-
tion*, Dionysius set out his ideals. 'A historian must, first of
all, select an attractive subject which will appeal to his read-
ers; secondly, he must know where to begin and where
to end; thirdly, he must know what to include and what
to leave out; fourthly, he must be careful to arrange his narrative in the correct order; finally, he must be impartial.'

When Dionysius reaches the long consecutive narrative of the Republic, these formal principles come very much into play. Events are divided, almost mechanically, into 'Domestic' and 'Foreign' and treated in strict sequence. Although he is very much concerned about the moral implications of history, his characters do not embody virtues and vices in the way that Livy's do. This is seen most evidently in the speeches which, however apocryphal, literary tradition required him to put into their mouths. On the whole these are perfect copy-book exercises, arguing the hypothetical pros and cons of a particular course of action, with standard arguments and standard allusions to the great models, Lysias, Demosthenes and Aeschines, but they do nothing to enliven the drama of the situation or to reveal the personality of the historical personage. It is this that makes Dionysius flat to read.

Livy's History of Rome from the foundation of the City to 9 BC (*Ab Urbe Condita*) comprised in all 142 books but of these only 1-10 and 21-45 survive. Apart from fragments, quoted by grammarians and others, and a short section dealing with the death of Cicero (Book 120), the other books are known only from summaries.

Internal evidence suggests that Livy began to write in or shortly before 29 BC by which time Octavian, the later Augustus, had restored peace and a measure of stability to the Roman world. A note in the Summary of Book 121 records that that book (and presumably those which followed) was published (*editus*) after Augustus' death in AD 14. The implication is that the last twenty books dealing with the events from the Battle of Actium until 9 BC were an afterthought to the original plan and were also too politically explosive to be published in Augustus' lifetime.

The sheer scope of the undertaking is formidable, presupposing, as it does, the composition of three Books a year on average. The introductions, especially to Books 6, 21 and 31, show that Livy began by composing and publishing in units of five books, the length of which was determined by the size of the ancient papyrus roll. As his material became more complex, this symmetrical pattern is less self-evident but it is likely that he maintained it.

Unlike his predecessors Livy was not a public figure. Whereas Q. Fabius Pictor, the elder Cato, L. Calpurnius Piso, C. Licinius Macer or Sallust himself, had all been active in politics, Livy, so far as we know, held no office and took no part in affairs. He was born in Padua in North Italy, probably in 59 BC, but established himself at Rome where he made the acquaintance of Augustus and acted for a time as a literary adviser to the future emperor Claudius. But his contacts with the Imperial House were personal and literary, not political or administrative. His life was spent as a writer and he died in Padua, not Rome, in AD 17. This inexperience had certain consequences. His exclusion from the Senate and the magistracies meant that he had no personal knowledge of how the Roman government worked and this ignorance shows itself from time to time in his work (as at 1.32.12, or 3.40.5). It also deprived him of first-hand access to much material (minutes of Senate-meetings, texts of treaties, laws, the records of the priestly colleges, etc.) which was preserved in official quarters. But the chief effect is that Livy did not seek historical explanations in political terms. For other Romans, history was a political study, through which one might hope to explain or excuse the past and the present, but Livy saw history in personal and moral terms. The purpose is clearly set out in his *Preface*:

I invite the reader's attention to the much more serious consideration of the kind of lives our ancestors lived, of who were the men and what the means, both in politics and war, by which Rome's power was first acquired and subsequently expanded: I would then have him trace the process of our moral decline, to watch first the sinking of the foundations of morality as the old teaching was allowed to lapse, then the final collapse of the whole edifice, and the dark dawning of our modern day when we can neither endure our vices nor face the remedies needed to cure them. The study of history is the best medicine for a sick mind; for in history you have a record of the infinite variety of human experience plainly set out for all to see: and in that record you can find for yourself and your country both examples and warnings.

Although Sallust and earlier historians had also adopted the outlook that morality was in steady decline and had argued that people do the sort of things that they do because they are the sort of people that they are, that is, have the moral character that they have, for Livy these beliefs were a matter of passionate concern. He saw history in terms of human personalities and representative individuals rather than of partisan politics. And his own experience, going back perhaps to his youth in Padua, made him feel the moral evils of his time with peculiar intensity. He punctuates his history with such revealing comments as 'fortunately in those days authority, both religious and secular, was still a guide to conduct and there was as yet no sign of our modern scepticism which interprets solemn compacts to suit its own convenience' (3.20.5).

Livy was content to have as a basis a narrative which he could elaborate and write up. What his practice was when dealing with contemporary history we are sadly unable to know, but with earlier history, certainly up to 100 BC, he selected the more recent historians and simply reshaped and rewrote their material.

His method was to follow one writer for a section, largely working from memory, and to switch to another when a particular theme had been exhausted. As an intelligent man he was indeed aware of the conflicts between his sources, and also of their individual prejudices, but he did not regard it as necessary or possible to unravel such discrepancies. A typical comment is (4.23.3.): 'When so much is veiled in antiquity this fact also may remain uncertain'.

Given therefore the assumption that the most important thing about history is that people have a certain inherited personality (*ingenium*, compare 3.36.1. Ap. Claudius) which determines their actions and that a historian can, even when the specific evidence is lacking, recreate how someone of a certain character would have behaved in any given set of circumstances, Livy's aim was to construct a meaningful series of scenes. To understand how he does this it is necessary to remember that he, like Dionysius of Halicarnassus and most of his contemporaries, had been educated along almost exclusively rhetorical lines. That education involved learning how to compose a speech (whether forensic or merely ceremonial) and a major stage in any such speech was the essential business of expounding in the simplest possible terms the basic facts that led up to the present situation. The *narratio*, as it was called, is analysed by all the leading exponents of rhetorical training (Cicero, *On the Orator* 122) and is perfected in such speeches as Cicero's *On behalf of Archias* (4-7). The requirements were three. A *narratio* should be brief (*brevis*), that is, it should not go into unnecessary preliminaries or diversions. It should be lucid (*aperta*), that is, it should be factually and chronologically coherent, even if this entailed the suppression or revision of some of the evidence. Above all, it should be plausible (*probabilis*), that is, in particular, the facts should be adjusted to the natures of the actors involved (*ad naturam eorum qui agent accommodabitur*).

It was this rhetorical background which enabled Livy, both on a practical level, to cope with the great undifferentiated mass of Roman historical happenings and, on a philosophical level, to make sense of it. The genre required of him that he should preserve to a large extent the annalistic framework, according to which, as in a chronicle, the events of every year were recorded, even down to the trivialities of prodigies and minor elections, but from these he selected certain topics which were inherently significant. In early Republican history this was relatively easy. Events were of a sufficiently short compass to form self-contained units in themselves. But even here Livy displayed his art of creating coherent episodes that revealed the character of the participants. Coriolanus, for instance, conducted his campaign against Rome over a number of years and led at least two separate expeditions against the walls of the City. In Livy's account two complete consular years are simply omitted and the two distinct expeditions are combined with a cheerful arbitrariness that makes as much geographical nonsense of the whole resulting narrative (2.33-40) as the two quite different routes combined for Hannibal's crossing of the Alps. But that narrative is, for the reader, brief, lucid and plausible and, therefore, as a work of art, carries its own conviction. When Livy came on to deal with more extended history, such as the Hannibalic and Macedonian wars, the problem was on a very much greater scale. Yet, even so, one can see his instinct at work in shaping the material into manageable units, such as the siege of Abydus in 200 BC (31.17-18). One unifying factor in this process was to single out the special quality of the protagonist. Thus his account of the reign of Tullus Hostilius centres on the king's *ferocia* (a word which, with its derivatives, occurs nine times in as many chapters) and the events are tailored to bring out that characteristic. So Camillus is built up as an example of *pietas*, an undistinguished soldier, Tempanius, as an example as much of moderation as of bravery (4.40-41). Hannibal, as a model of perfidy and impetuosity, or Flaminius, Polybius' very different picture of him makes very clear, as a sympathetic and phil-hellene man of action. On a wider scale, the siege of Abydus is told in terms of madness (*rabies*, a word which occurs three times in Livy's account and for which there is no prompting in his source, Polybius). History was, for Livy, a psychological record.

But the enormous field of history which he had set himself to cover raised further problems. How was the interest of the reader to be sustained over all 142 Books? Quintilian characterized his style as possessing a 'milky richness' (19.1.32, *lactea ubertas*) which might be thought to imply the measured pace of a Gibbon; but, in fact, Livy is remarkable for the extreme range of styles which he uses in his narrative in order to achieve variety. At one moment, when recounting essentially perfunctory details he will use a matter-of-fact style, with stock vocabulary and the minimum of syntactical subordination, and then will write a series of complicated sentences which set out the preliminary dispositions, often with participial clauses explaining the motives and thoughts of the chief figures. The action will be described in the stereotyped language of a military communiqué (especially the use of the impersonal passive) or short, staccato sentences, employing the historic infinitive or historic present. Finally, in describing the climax or its aftermath, Livy will allow his language to be coloured with words which (such was the particularity of the Latin stylistic tradition) could normally only have been used in heroic poetry. A terse comment – *haec eo anno acta* 'this happened that year' – will round off the episode. By this variation Livy was able to convey an impression not only of the military facts but also of the emotional experience of the participants.

If Livy's concern was to see history as the literary embodiment of individuals, then his success depended to a very large extent on making those historical characters come alive, sound authentic. Earlier historians, such as Thucydides, had been criticized for putting speeches into the mouths of their leading characters which did not truly bring out their individuality, but Livy, as he himself says, was able to enter into the spirit of his characters (43.13.2. *mihi vetustas res scribenti nescio quo pacto antiquus fit animus*). The climax of any episode is often a passage of direct or indirect speech, which characterizes the chief actor. Sometimes the idiom will be coarse and colloquial if the speakers are lower class. For example, a rough citizen (1.50.7. *seditiosus facinerosusque homo*) inveighs against Tarquinius Superbus in a bitter repartee which includes the word *infortunium*, 'hard luck', not found elsewhere in classical prose authors but common in the slave-talk of Plautus and Terence. Or some embittered tribunes of the people complain that the patricians thwart their ambitions at every turn (4.35.5-11) using several expressions found also only in colloquial context (e.g. *sugillari*, 'to rebuff', *praebere os*, 'to expose oneself to'). Sometimes when the occasion is one of high drama Livy will allow his speakers to use language more associated with poetry than prose. Thus the climax of the story of Coriolanus is the great scene with his mother at the gates of Rome. She speaks to him, as Jocasta to her sons in Greek tragedy, and her speech contains several unique features which stamp it as tragic (2.40.5-7): *sino*, 'I allow', with the subjunctive rather than the accusative and infinitive, *quamuis*, 'although', with the indicative (only here in Livy), the rare *senecta* for *senectus*, 'old age', the phrase *ira cecidit*, 'anger subsided', found elsewhere only in the poets.

A modern scholar has perpetually to be on his guard against such almost subliminal deception. The narrative, as given by Livy or Dionysius, has to be ruthlessly scrutinized for signs of anachronism or embellishment. What is left is the hard core on which a new reconstruction can be attempted with the aid of the chance survivals through other literary sources or through archaeology. It is this which the following chapters try to achieve.

3 *The Arrival of the Etruscans*

The turning point in the rise of any nation or civilization comes when scattered families are drawn together and form a town or city. Then, for the first time, every member of the community can put his special skills to the maximum use.

The Etruscans came to Rome and settled in force – as craftsmen, merchants, builders, religious experts, doctors, and rulers. It was not a case of an alien usurpation of the throne for a temporary period: it was a deep interpenetration of society at every level. Before the Etruscans there were communities at Rome: their arrival created, but not overnight, a homogeneous city which blended the different cultural elements into one.

The Romans thought of the Etruscans as great town-planners who laid out their cities on a carefully surveyed grid-system, and with precise attention to religious protocol (Festus 358L.), just as their military engineers attributed the formal design of a Roman camp to the same Etruscan model. Religious observances there certainly were, especially the sacred furrow that was driven round the area to be enclosed by a city (*pomerium*) and only intermitted where a gate was to be situated. But Etruscan cities are not, in fact, very mathematical in design, largely because conditions of geography or history did not allow for such uncompromising rigidity. Veii, it is true, is fairly symmetrical, with streets radiating from a centre, but other towns, such as Vetulonia, were built on steep and uneven ground. The only clear example, still unexcavated, is Marzobotto, where air photographs have revealed a very clear grid-system. But Marzobotto is late, *c.* 500 BC, and reflects the influence of a Greek art that was to be perfected by Hippodamus of Miletus.

The Etruscans were, *par excellence*, city-dwellers and their arrival at Rome and their fusion with the native population radically changed the whole character of the settlement. From an agglomeration of dwelling-huts it became an architectural city, with streets, public buildings, markets, shops, temples, and domestic houses. This transition did not occur overnight, as some scholars, notably Gjerstad, have argued. Gjerstad, indeed, basing his argument on the fact that the area of the Forum appears to have been floored in a permanent fashion for the first time *c.* 575 BC, dates the whole Etruscan penetration of Rome from that date. In fact from 625 to 575 BC Etruscan ideas can be seen spreading in Rome. This is shown chiefly by contemporary pottery which is either influenced by Etruscan styles or is actually of Etruscan manufacture. From the same period, moreover, roof-tiles have been recovered, proving that the thatched huts were beginning to give way to houses of brick, stucco and tile. The decisive step in the evolution of the city was to turn the Forum area into a central focus which unified the separate hill-communities. There were two prerequisites before this could be done: first, the low-lying ground had to be adequately drained and, secondly, it had to be freed from use as a burial ground. There is evidence of serious flooding *c.* 625 BC and it is likely that the first serious drainage works followed soon after. The great drain (Cloaca Maxima), in reality a large open ditch, was attributed to the last Tarquin but this only represents an improvement on earlier attempts. The Etruscans were, as is becoming increasingly clear, the great water engineers of their time. The massive *cuniculi* or drainage tunnels which have been found in their hundreds in S. Etruria are eloquent testimony of this (Plate 7), apart from traditional stories, such as how the Romans entered Veii by a *cuniculus* or how the Alban lake was regulated by a tunnel. It is, therefore, natural to attribute the drainage of the Forum-area to their initiative. Secondly, burials in the area seem to stop by 600 BC, indicating that it was already being recognized as a public centre. Rome, therefore, was beginning to grow into an urbanized community by the beginning of the sixth century; and further proof of this lies in the fact that the first road-bed of the key street which ran through the heart of the city, the Sacred Way, dates in all probability from before 575 BC. One of the most important religious shrines of Rome – the Regia or Royal Palace, which was never a residence but contained the sanctuary of Mars – was also in the Forum area. It has been the subject of meticulous investigation by Professor F. Brown whose conclusions are that the first cult building on the site (replacing earlier huts and burials) dates from the end of the seventh century. It consisted of a stone-founded precinct and stone-walled enclosure containing a monument of unknown kind. It was, in its turn, replaced, in the second quarter of the sixth century, by a more recognizable (if short-lived) temple.

In other words, we should try to visualize the gradual transformation and expansion of Rome from the late seventh century into a fully-fledged city by the time of the last king. It was a haphazard and unplanned business. Open-air sanctuaries were gradually replaced by more impressive temples. Thus, the Cattle Market (Forum Boarium), which was laid out *c*. 575 BC and contained at least one open altar, had, by the beginning of the fifth century, been embellished with twin temples (dedicated to Fortune and Mater Matuta). The primary institutions of Rome began to acquire their lasting and permanent homes. The House of the Vestal Virgins in the Forum has yielded a rubbish-pit with fragments of pottery dating back to about 600 BC. The Temple of Vesta itself has votive deposits extending from *c*. 575 BC down to much later times. Conditions for excavations in Rome are extremely difficult and it is often only through chance discoveries that knowledge can be obtained. The literary sources, for instance, speak of the elder Tarquin making land available for private builders to construct shops (*tabernae*) near the Forum (Livy 1.35.10). No trace of them survives; yet they are a natural and inevitable concomitant of the two big market-places (the Forum and the Forum Boarium) which were laid out. No doubt it is mere accident that nothing has been found of them in a city that has been so continually rebuilt and so continuously inhabited. Again, the sources speak of the Tarquins laying out the Circus Maximus. The existing remains have not revealed any specifically Etruscan or sixth-century evidence, but we know from elsewhere how prominent a place the games filled in the lives of the Etruscans, and need have no hesitation in believing the written tradition.

By the time of the last Tarquin, Rome was a city. It had its public monuments, soon to be overtopped by the great temple of Jupiter Optimus Maximus; it had its markets and shops; it had its streets and its drains; it had its houses and its Curial halls; it had its place where the people could assemble to discuss politics or to engage in the religious activity of sport. It had indeed become what one ancient writer called a Greek city. Yet this was entirely due to the unpredictable combination of Etruscan urban architecture with native Latin roots.

New Rome – the result of the fusion of Etruscan and native – became recognizably a city; it also acquired some of the features which characterized Greek city-states and distinguished them from other less-civilized communities, in particular a well-defined legendary past, a carefully formulated religion and a disciplined citizen army.

But a city, like any other organization, needs some common symbol through which it can assert its common identity. The Union Jack, the Stars and Stripes, the Crown, the Cross – all in their different ways help to unite people and give them a sense of belonging. For Greek and Roman people this symbol was the story of the founding of their nation or city.

Rome was fortunate enough to have two foundation legends – Romulus and Remus, and Aeneas. Although the Romulus legend was much embroidered over the centuries under the influence of Greek mythology, it is generally regarded as being in essence very ancient. H. Strasburger has indeed recently tried to date its main formation to the early third century BC as part of the propaganda of the Samnite and Pyrrhic wars, but this is impossibly late. Aeneas, on the other hand, raises much more interesting problems because he links Rome with the Homeric world and the world of Greek civilization. He gave Rome international status, and that again was part of the Etruscan contribution to the rise of Rome.

Aeneas had survived the fall of Troy and had escaped. His survival, part of the Homeric tradition (*Iliad* 20. 215-240), was the basis from which his future wanderings were elaborated. As Greek knowledge of the western Mediterranean expanded, so Aeneas was made to venture farther afield, until by the early fifth century he had reached central Italy. There are two independent sources of evidence which indicate that towards the end of the sixth century he had been accepted as

E.R.E.

the founder-hero of Rome as of other Etruscan cities.

1. The first line is the evidence of Greek historians. The earliest explicit mention is in Hellanicus' *The Priestesses of Hera at Argos* (FGH 4F 84: *c.* 450 BC): 'Aeneas, coming from the land of the Molossians, founded Rome with Odysseus'. (It is not absolutely certain whether Hellanicus wrote 'after' or 'with' Odysseus but the latter is far more probable). He called it Rome after the name of one of the Trojan women, Rhome, who had accompanied him. This version was adopted by another Greek historian, Damastes of Sigeum (FGH 5 F 3 : *c.* 400 BC), and by several other Greek writers, if we may believe the word of a much later scholar, Dionysius of Halicarnassus, who claims to have consulted them (1.72.2). In other words, in the sixth and fifth century the Greeks were sufficiently impressed by the size and importance of Rome to invest it with the respectability of Greek associations. But essentially Hellanicus represents a Greek view of Rome rather than Roman aspirations to a Hellenic connection.

2. The second line, however, is evidence from Etruscan archaeology. The theme of Aeneas' departure with Anchises was a popular artistic theme. It is depicted on a large number of Attic vases dating from 525-470 BC. Fifty-eight vases (fifty-two black-figure, five red-figure and one Etruscan red-figure [from Vulci]) have so far been identified with this motif, and at least seventeen of these, probably many more, were found in Etruria; but these statistics need to be treated with caution. Aeneas also appears on other vases and other works of art in different roles – as warrior, and accomplice of Paris, just as often as refugee setting off to found a new city. But there is more unambiguous evidence. At Veii a number of votive statuettes of Aeneas carrying Anchises have been found (Plate 4). They date from the period 515-490 and can only indicate that there was a cult of Aeneas in the city then. Further evidence is provided by a sixth-century Etruscan scarab also showing Aeneas carrying the sacra of Troy and Anchises. If this evidence is considered as a whole, it points to the popularity of Aeneas as a founder-hero in S. Etruria towards the end of the sixth century, especially at Veii and Vulci. There has been much dispute how the Aeneas legend was transmitted to Etruria, whether from Sicily or Campania

or directly from Greece itself, but this does not affect the main argument.

There is no such archaeological evidence as yet for Rome itself, but Rome now united Latin and Etruscan elements, as the author of the lines at the end of Hesiod's *Theogony* (1011-6: written about 520-500 BC) recognizes: 'Circe, the daughter of the Sun, bore, as children to Odysseus, Agrius and stout-hearted Latinus, who ruled over all the noble Tyrrhenians [Etruscans] far off in a quiet corner of holy islands.'

It is, therefore, legitimate to argue that during the last years of the Tarquin supremacy at Rome, the Etruscan view of Aeneas as a founder-hero and the Greek view of Aeneas as the explorer of the west coalesced at Rome (and elsewhere) to produce a foundation legend for the city. How Rome came to acquire a monopoly of Aeneas, how his mythical connection with neighbouring Latin cities, especially Lavinium and Alba, grew up over the succeeding centuries, and how the chronological complication resulting from an attempt to harmonize the rival legends of Aeneas (traditionally *c.* 1175 BC) and Romulus (traditionally *c.* 750 BC) were resolved are intriguing questions but lie outside the period of this study. The relevant point is that as Rome evolved into a city, so she acquired a pedigree of the noblest descent.

The foundation legend was one uniting bond, but another was the coming together of all men and women at Rome in common religious worship, which focused their needs and aspirations in a single approach.

Early Roman religion is extremely shadowy. As far as we know it was aniconic (that is, it did not have images of gods) and certainly not anthropomorphic. It was a faith which sought to understand how the processes of nature operated and to establish a working relationship with them. It was based on a practical core of prayer and sacrifice.

In common with many Italic people, the primitive Romans worshipped Mars as their chief deity. Mars and Ops (but not Jupiter) had a sanctuary in the Regia; Mars, together with Jupiter and Quirinus, formed an ancient triad, served by the three chief priests (*flamines*) and worshipped on the Quirinal (cf. Varro, *On the Latin Language* 5.158; CIL. 6.438,

475, 565); Mars was the god who presided over the purification of the fields (Ambarvalia), of the city (Amburbium) and
the citizen-body (the five-yearly *lustrum*). Mars stands at the
head of the foundation legend as the divine father of Romulus
and Remus (Livy 1.4.1-3). It was to Mars that a horse was
sacrificed on the Ides of October. The list could be extended of
the survivals which show Mars as the central god, just as he
was for the people of Iguvium, in northern Italy, part of
whose ritual has been preserved in inscriptions (the Iguvine
Tables) and for other Italic races, such as the Marri, Marru-
cini and Mamertini who bear his name.

The role of Mars as the principal god of early Rome has
been disputed. Scholars have been divided between seeing
him as a war-god (Dumézil) or as a vegetation god (Mann-
hardt, Warde-Fowler) and have constructed connections between these two functions. The war-god attributes derive
largely from the identification made, at least by the third century BC, with the Greek Ares and with his custody of certain
ritual objects such as the ceremonial shields (*ancilia*) and
spears which were kept in the Regia. If the spears of Mars
shook of their own accord, as they did in 99 BC, it was an ill
omen (Aul. Gell. 4.6.2). When war was declared the chief
magistrate went to the Regia and shook the shields with the
cry 'Mars, awake' (*Mars, vigila*) (Serv. on *Aeneid.* 8.3). Yet as a
war-god Mars is quite colourless apart from Ares and even in
the guise of Ares never acquired any distinction. Phrases such
as *aequo Marte* (indecisive battle) are conventional and purely
literary. On the other hand Mars obviously does figure strongly
in agricultural contexts – in prayers, for instance, quoted by
the elder Cato in his work on Farming. And Mars is associated
with the rite and powers of fertility (e.g. Ops). The two conflicting aspects can only be reconciled if they are seen as
parallel activities of a god whose chief function is as pro-
tector of the whole people. In a very old invocation, preserved by Aulus Gellius (13.23.2), the attribute of Mars is given
as *Nerio*, which seems to mean simply 'manliness'. The
strength of Mars – his power to protect – is linked with the
cleansing power (Lua) of Saturn and the springiness (Salacia)
of Neptune (water).

But Mars remained indistinct. Only his sacred emblems and

his ceremonies served to establish his prominence. The Etruscans brought with them more vigorous ideas. They personalized their gods, they thought of them visually and they housed them in temples instead of merely dedicating altars to them. In this they owed something to Greek influence and something to their own vivid imaginations. Their chief god was Tinia – the great sky-god – a fine representation of whose head has been discovered at Satricum, near Rome. He came to share much of the prestige and qualities of the Greek Zeus. It is, therefore, no surprise that one of the crowning architectural glories of the Tarquin dynasty was the construction of a huge temple to Jupiter 'The Sky-Father', together with Juno (Etr. *uni*) and Minerva (Etr. *menrva*). The temple itself belongs to the very end of the sixth century (see p. 84) but the cult may have begun in an open sanctuary (*locus sacer sine tecto*), as so many did. This Capitoline triad superseded the earlier supremacy of Mars and the older triad of Mars, Jupiter and Quirinus. Jupiter Optimus Maximus (Best and Greatest) became the patron deity of Rome and came to occupy the central place in the religious life of the city. It was to him that sacrifice was made by the chief magistrates on entering office. His cult-statue was fabricated in terracotta by a great sculptor, Vulca of Veii, and was set in the middle shrine, clothed in an embroidered tunic and toga, for all to see and worship.

Another indication of how the Etruscan Jupiter Optimus Maximus supplanted the earlier gods of Rome is provided by the history of the Roman triumph.

There was an archaic ceremony whereby a victorious general dedicated a trophy consisting of the armour of a defeated enemy at the shrine of Jupiter Feretrius. This was a primitive shrine on the Capitol whose origins, like the significance of the cult-title Feretrius, are lost in mystery. The procedure was described by Varro who cites a 'Law of Numa' (Festus 204L.) as evidence which, at the least, establishes a very ancient date for it, and it has parallels from other cultures. But it was so antiquated by the historical age of Rome that there was wide disagreement about the particular details. It is generally reported that there were three trophies – *spolia opima prima, secunda, tertia* – and that they were

offered to Jupiter Feretrius, Mars and (Janus) Quirinus respectively, that is the original triad described above. But
the precise distinction escapes our knowledge. Some scholars
hold that the *spolia* were dedicated in turn to all three deities
by stages on the same occasion, as the procession moved
through Rome. Others argue that the difference was based
upon the standing of the commander, a consul, commanding
with full power, making his offering to Jupiter while lesser
commanders made theirs to the other two gods. A third
view, supported by Servius, the commentator on Vergil, holds
that there were only three such dedications in the course of
Rome's history – the first by Romulus to Jupiter, the second
by Cossus (in 437 BC) to Mars (see p. 142) and the third by Marcellus (in 222 BC) to Quirinus. This last view is certainly
mistaken, but it is true that the ceremony was superseded by
the triumph in historical times and that only Cossus and
Marcellus revived it after 500 BC.

The victorious general was granted by the Senate the privilege of entering Rome in a chariot and processing to the
temple of Jupiter Optimus Maximus. In the fully developed
form of the triumph, he wore a special purple (or, later,
embroidered) *toga*, he wore a wreath, his face was painted
red and he held a sceptre. Before him marched his prisoners,
accompanied by the spoils and other exhibits. Behind him in
his chariot stood a servant who repeated 'Remember that
you are a man!' The ceremony was one of the most colour-
ful in Rome and was an honour passionately sought after
– even by Cicero.

The date of the institution of the ceremony cannot be
exactly established. The first specific allusion to a triumph
concerns the elder Tarquin (Livy 1.33.3) who returned
triumphans from his conquest of the neighbouring Latium,
but this can hardly be regarded as historical and all that can
be said is that the ceremony must belong closely with the
institution of the cult of Jupiter Optimus Maximus. This is
borne out by the fact that equivalent scenes are represented on
contemporary Etruscan monuments. Equal uncertainty surrounds the precise significance to be given to the appearance
of the triumphator. Was he for a day identified with Jupiter
himself? Or was he acting as king and were later trium-

phators recreating the role and dress of the king? Or both?

At first sight the triumphator's red paint, his wearing of the dress of Jupiter (*ornatus Iovis*) and the warning of the slave behind him point to the divine explanation. And there are Greek parallels for this. So too the ritual cry *io, triumpe* has been interpreted as a call on the god to manifest himself. But which god? The word triumph must be connected with, and could be derived from, the Greek *Thriambos* which is a cult name of Dionysus. But Dionysus does not figure in the Roman pantheon as early as 500 BC. The god Triumph occurs in the art and poetry of the late Republic but, like almost all such abstracts, he too is not a primitive concept. Only Jupiter remains. On the other hand Etruscan monuments regularly depict men in the same dress, and some scholars, comparing *tripudium* 'a three-beat dance step' interpret the cry '*triumpe*' rather as an exhortation to dance. There have recently been two compromise solutions. Versnel, in a thorough study (*Triumphus*, 1970), claims that the triumphator was characterized both as god and king. The victorious king, who possessed divinity by virtue of his position and power, made a ceremonial entry into the city to renew its prosperity and fortune, just as New Year rituals designed to renew the annual life of nature involve a ceremonial entrance. L. Bonfante Warren independently argued that nothing could be inferred from the triumphator's appearance because king or tyrant, triumphator or god were simply dressed in contemporary Etruscan manner. The identity is no more than an identity of fashion, without any of the implications of divinity. It was only later, under Roman influence, that these outward marks acquired religious symbolism.

Now it is certainly true that we have very little contemporary evidence for what a fifth-century triumph was like. All our sources are later, and the representations are ambiguous. The triumph must have undergone changes, particularly when the Romans came into contact with the Hellenistic world and were impressed by Dionysiac processions with their luxury and splendour. From now on the general was indeed regarded as a god and fêted as such. The military successes of Alexander and his gradual transformation into Dionysus also contributed to this elaboration. Dr S. Weinstock,

in his profound study of the religious achievements of Julius
Caesar, indeed goes so far as to hold that most of what were
later regarded as the specifically divine attributes of the
triumph may have been introduced well after 250 BC and precedents fabricated to justify them in the more remote past.
Camillus, for example, was alleged to have used white horses
to pull his chariot at his triumph to celebrate the capture of
Veii in 396 BC (p. 158). White horses, above all, signify
divinity. They pulled the chariots of Zeus and Helios. They
pulled the chariot of Julius Caesar. But there is nothing historical about Camillus' white horses: they were part of a
subsequent legend evolved in the time of the Scipios. Nor
have we any absolute proof that the early triumphators
wore red paint: this, again, is ascribed to Camillus (Pliny,
Natural History, 33.111). Weinstock concludes that the triumphator was originally just the king but over the centuries he
evolved into a mystical and divine figure, culminating in the
exaltation of Caesar in 46 BC.

Certainty is clearly impossible and, no doubt, attitudes to
the triumph did change over the centuries as different
features received different emphasis. I myself believe that the
divine identification was a part of the original Etruscan
ceremony but that it was subsequently much modified and
enhanced. We know little if anything of Etruscan theology,
except that its debt to Greece was substantial in some details.
And in Greece the return of a successful athletic victor to his
home-town, in a chariot and through a special entrance, was
regarded as as near to apotheosis as one could decently get
(Plutarch, *Quaest. Conv.* 2.5.2; cf. Pindar, *Pythian Odes*,
10.22ff.). In 412 BC Exaenetus, an Olympic victor, returned to
Acragas in a four-horse chariot, accompanied by 300 young
men (Diodorus, 13.82.7).

One other decisive religious innovation deserves notice, if
only because its influence has lasted down to our times. The
calendar, as reformed by Julius Caesar, was a hybrid affair.
Previously it had been a makeshift lunisolar calendar of
355 days which, theoretically, was brought back to true by
the periodic insertion of an extra month of twenty-seven

days. Caesar added ten days to the year, at the end of the
shorter months, bringing the total up to 365, which is a
reasonable approximation to the solar year, and introducing
the leap-year to make the adjustment complete. The previous calendar is known both from literary evidence and
from one largely surviving inscription (the Fasti Antiates
Maiores). Its compromise character is revealed by the fact
that a true lunar calendar would have had twenty-nine or
thirty days in a month, but the pre-Julian calendar had four
months of thirty-one days, seven of twenty-nine and one
(February) of twenty-eight; and the periodic adjustment to
the solar year by reducing February to twenty-three or
twenty-four days and adding an extra month of twenty-seven,
implies knowledge of the length of the solar year.

The implication is that there must originally have been a
purely lunar calendar which at some stage was modified in
a rough and ready way to bring it into conformity with the
solar cycle. This is borne out by the division of the Roman
month into Kalends (1st), Nones (5th or 7th) and Ides (13th
or 15th). Macrobius (*Sat.* 1.15.19), a fifth-century AD scholar
using much older sources, records that before the Kalends a
priest was given the task of watching for the crescent moon
and announcing its appearance to the Rex (King). Similarly the
Nones would be the first quarter and the Ides the full moon.
All these details substantiate the belief that the original regal
calendar was a typical lunar calendar, of 355 days. And this
is indeed what some of the ancient scholars themselves
record, giving the credit to King Numa, as was usual since
he attracted to himself all religious innovations. Thus Fulvius
Nobilior, who was consul in 189 BC and who wrote a commentary on the calendar, expressly stated that Numa created
a 355-day year (Censorinus, *de Die Natali* 20).

The revolutionary change was, then, the move from a
purely lunar calendar of 355 days to one which, while still
preserving some of the features of a lunar calendar, was essentially geared to a solar year.

But the other notable feature of the Roman calendar, and in
particular of the one extant example which survives from
before Julius Caesar's reforms, is that each day is distinguished

in two ways: first by a letter signifying the religious character of that day (C=*comitialis*, on which *comitia* or assemblies
could be held; F=*fastus*, on which legal business could be
transacted but assemblies could not be held, N=*nefastus*, on
which neither legal business nor assemblies could take place:
in addition there are some rarer signs of which the most important for the present purpose is QRCF (Quando Rex Comiti-
avit Fas=a *fastus dies* when the King has held the assembly);
and secondly by a notice recording what religious festival
falls on that day. In this pre-Julian calendar (the Fasti
Antiates Maiores) some of these festivals are inscribed in
large capital letters, while others, of clearly later origin, are
painted in smaller, red letters. It used to be assumed that
because of the mention of the king in QRCF and because of
the antiquity of the large-letter festivals, we have here a true
survival of the genuine Etruscan regal calendar. Unfortunately
the answer cannot be quite as simple as that, since some of
the festivals, e.g. the Cerealia and the Lucaria, must be later
than 510 BC. The cult of Ceres was only instituted in 496 BC
and the traditional explanation of the Lucaria connects it with
the concealment of some Roman fugitives in a grove (*lucus*)
after their defeat by the Gauls at the Battle of the Allia (390
BC). I doubt whether this explanation is based on anything substantial, but the Cerealia is conclusive in itself.

The Etruscans had links with the Near East which had developed lunisolar calendars, whereas the Greeks never did so.
Despite the persuasive arguments of Mrs Michels, I am con-
vinced that the adoption of this hybrid lunisolar calendar was
carried through during the Etruscan kingdom at Rome, but
that it was only openly published, for all to see, read and
understand, some three generations later, during the time of
the Decemvirate (p. 118) when popular clamour succeeded in
opening many files and in disclosing many of the secret acts
of government. This would account for the presence in the
established calendar of some later festivals such as the
Cerealia, which had been incorporated between the expulsion
of the kings and the Decemvirate.

Whatever the precise answer, the calendar both gave Rome
a day-to-day framework for an efficient administration and
also enabled her to compete on equal terms with the most

advanced and civilized cities and countries of the time.

Rome grew great because of her military power – and this again was a consequence of the interaction between Etruscan and native. Nothing is known of the Roman militia before Etruscan influence began to infiltrate it, unless the dancing warrior-priests, the Salii, perpetuated the memory of primitive armour and primitive methods. They were armed with a distinctive figure-of-eight shield (*ancile*), a bronze breast-plate, a helmet (*apex*), and long sword (Dionysius 2.70). All these pieces of armour have their counterparts in the late Bronze Age, particularly in Mycenaean culture, and represent a style of fighting very different from the organized tactics of a mass infantry battle. They are the weapons of a 'heroic' age. But no other trace of them has been found at Rome and there is no literary evidence of value to describe how the Romans of the eighth century BC fought.

It is only with the Etruscans that we begin to discern a planned army, but the difficulties in reconstructing it are formidable. The central fact, however, is that there were two stages of development. The second stage, associated with the name of Servius Tullius, was the revolutionary one by which new weapons and so, ultimately, new tactics were adopted, which transferred the balance of strength from the cavalry to the infantry and which required a larger reservoir of recruits selected for their financial means. It was the Servian army that, despite all the transformations down the centuries, remained the tool of Roman success.

The first stage is more obscure. From very early times there survived the name of three groups of people – Ramnenses (or Ramnes), Titienses (or Tities) and Luceres. Two quite separate explanations of these names were given: 1. Varro (*On the Latin Language* 5.46, 55) argued that they were the names of the original tribes at Rome, as instituted by Romulus and called after his supporters; 2. Livy (1.13.6-8; cf. Cicero, *On the Republic* 2.36) says that they were the names of the three squadrons, each 100 strong, of cavalry formed by Romulus. One thing is certain, as Varro's source, the poet Volnius, saw: all three names are Etruscan. They can, therefore, have nothing to do with Romulus. Of the two alternative explanations Livy's is historically the more likely. Varro's represents an attempt to minimize the influence of the Etruscan domination of Rome and a desire to invent a plausibly mathematical history of the Roman tribes (see p. 54). There was an independent tradition that Romulus created 300 Celeres – or cavalry (Festus 48L.; Pliny, *Natural History* 33-35; Servius, *on Aeneid* 9.368: other sources identify the Celeres with the King's personal bodyguard); and it is likely that the Celeres are the same as the Ramnenses, Titienses and Luceres, and have been wrongly retrojected from early Etruscan times to the mythical age of Romulus. Again, according to a tradition associated with the myth of a great Etruscan augur, Attus Navius (Livy 1.36.3ff.; Cicero, *On Divination* 1.33; Dionysius 3.71.1; Festus 452 L.), the number of cavalry centuries (squadrons of 100) was doubled to six under the first Tarquin and named, respectively, *Ramnenses priores* and *posteriores*, etc. This again looks like speculation. The natural meaning of *priores* and *posteriores* is not 'earlier' and 'later' but 'front' and 'back' – implying their relative positions on parade, just as in the later legion there were centurions *prioris centuriae* and *posterioris centuriae* (Livy 42.34). Six squadrons of cavalry took part in the very ancient religious ceremony called the Transvectio Equorum.

The assumption then is that near the beginning of the sixth century the Roman army consisted chiefly of an effective cavalry force of 600, supported by a less important infantry arm ranging from light-armed skirmishers to well-equipped soldiers, like those whose burials, containing a round-shield, swords and breast-plates, have been discovered on the Esquiline, dating from the late seventh century. This was the army that made possible the early expansion of Rome and the annexation of communities in the immediate vicinity of the city (see p. 73). Such an army would have been typical of many cities up and down the peninsula.

But already a change was making itself felt. The Greeks, from c.750 BC, had begun to develop heavy infantry armour, partly under Assyrian influence, partly, perhaps, from contact with metal-workers of Central Europe. The development was slow and piece-meal, but it was none the less epoch-making. The chief features of it were the adoption of a round shield carried on the left arm with an arm-band and a hand-grip, defensive metal body-armour (corslet, greaves, closed helmet), and a thrusting as opposed to a throwing spear. This was called by the Greeks hoplite armour. It led inexorably towards close-formation fighting, even though the evidence from Greece indicates that the perfection of the hoplite phalanx was 50-100 years later than the first appearance of hoplite weapons. The advanced technology spread through the Greeks to the Etruscans. There is a fine series of pre-hoplite shields from Etruria which continues down to about 650 BC. Thereafter the hoplite shield begins to appear, in actual finds (as at Fabriano) and on vase-paintings. In the sixth century the hoplite panoply is standard throughout Etruria.

There is no such conclusive archaeological evidence for Rome itself, but it is, a priori, unlikely that Etruscan Rome lagged far behind the rest of Etruria in such important military reforms. And there is other evidence. Servius Tullius, traditionally King from about 550 BC, was associated universally with the assessment of Roman citizens by wealth in order to provide a levy (legio) for fighting purposes. The surviving documents (Livy 1.43; Dionysius 4.16; Cicero, *On the Republic* 2.39) are unquestionably anachronistic when they specify five classes graded by wealth and equipped with different weapons, because money was not used earlier than the fourth century at Rome, and the assortment of armour prescribed is too bizarre and haphazard for belief. The document in Livy is interesting as a typical piece of pseudo-antiquarianism:

Out of those who had a rating of 100,000 asses or more he made 80 centuries, 40 each of seniors and of juniors; these were all known as the first class: the seniors were to be ready to guard the city, the juniors to wage war abroad. The armour which those men were required to provide consisted of helmet, round shield, greaves and breast-plate, all of bronze, for the protection of their bodies; their attacking weapons were a spear and a sword. There were added to this class two centuries of mechanics, who were to serve without arms; to them was entrusted the duty of making siege-engines in war. The second class was drawn up from those whose rating was between 100,000 and 75,000 asses; of these, seniors and juniors, 20 centuries were enrolled. The arms prescribed for them were an oblong shield in place of the round one and everything else except for the breast-plate as in the class above.

And so on for all five classes. There is, however, evidence for an earlier stage which divided the citizen-body into two, the *classis* (those eligible for military service on grounds of wealth) and those *infra classem*. This simple distinction, known from antiquarian sources (Festus 100L.; Aul. Gell. 6.13) is confirmed by a garbled historical notice in Livy of an engagement at Fidenae in which the *classis* (hardly the fleet) took part in 426 BC (4.34.6). The five-fold division of classes belongs to a much more sophisticated era.

How large the original Servian levy was is perhaps beyond conjecture. There is no reason to doubt that it was organized on units of 100 men (centuries) and towards the end of the fifth century it seems to have varied between 4,000 and 6,000 men: such figures square with the best estimates that can be made of Rome's population. 6,000 may have been the nominal maximum for Servius too, because Rome went through a long period of recession in the early fifth century when man-power would also have declined. If so, the Servian *classis* would have comprised sixty centuries. But we cannot know this. He may have started with a levy of only thirty or forty centuries. But whatever its size, the new army marked a radical break with the past, chiefly because of the priority which it gave to infantry over cavalry. This is one of the most hotly disputed issues in early Roman history but the balance of argument does suggest that the old cavalry now became subordinate, militarily and politically, to the hoplites, even if the rigorous discipline and tactics of a regular hoplite army were still a long way in the future. The evidence can be summarized.

1. The Servian military organization also acquired political significance (p. 64) and the six centuries of cavalry were known as the Sex Suffragia or Six Votes (voting units). Nevertheless if one thing is certain about the voting arrangements

of the whole Servian organization, it is that the Sex Suffragia voted *after* the hoplite *classis* (Cicero, *Philippic* 2.82). This can only imply that their importance was regarded as secondary.

2. In the early years after the fall of the Tarquin dynasty, the Romans occasionally met crises by suspending their normal constitution and appointing a special commander, *dictator or magister populi*, as he was called (p. 88). He had as his deputy a Master of Horse (*magister equitum*) and he himself was not allowed by religious protocol to ride a horse Plutarch, *Fabius* 4). Again the priorities are evident.

3. The decisive battle of the early Republic, Lake Regillus in c.496 BC, was coloured in its telling by much Homeric romanticism; but one historical circumstance emerges from the mist. According to tradition, the dictator, A. Postumius Albus, vowed a temple to the Dioscuri during the course of the battle. The Dioscuri were always thought of as the protectors of cavalry; they were represented with their horses in a statuary group near their temple in the Forum; an ancient ceremony – the passage of the cavalry (*transvectio equorum*) – was associated with their cult (Dionysius 6.13-4). Now the Dioscuri were not merely the patrons of Rome's enemies in that battle (p. 99): they symbolized the main fighting arm of the enemy – the cavalry. In vowing a temple to them Postumius was, therefore, attempting to persuade them to change sides. The implication is clear. By comparison with the Latins, Rome was weak in cavalry: her main strength lay now in her infantry.

The new hoplite army need not, however, have adopted at once hoplite tactics, which demand great steadiness and careful training. By the end of the fifth century, in the major wars against Veii and the Gauls, they certainly had become standard practice. Livy tells of a dictator, A. Postumius Tubertus, who in c.432 BC put his son to death for leaping from the ranks to attack the enemy (4.29). The punishment was deserved because the whole hoplite formation was put in jeopardy as soon as any break occurred in it. But forty-five years earlier, the Fabii went out to Cremera as a clan, with their clients, and this presupposes that they were not organized and trained as a hoplite phalanx. Too much, however, should not be built on this legend, for the whole story is so coloured by the Herodotean account of the 300 at Thermopylae that one cannot place much credence on any of the details. In any case the Fabii went out to provide a border-garrison in order to prevent Veientane encroachment on Roman land. They were in no sense a characteristic fighting force.

In general, however, the sporadic and guerrilla nature of the warfare in the early fifth century – against Sabines, Aequi, Volsci and Hernici, all marauding hill-people – suited a flexible military organization. It was only when Rome came up against organized armies that the precise tactics had to be formulated. The nucleus was already there, to be expanded as circumstances required.

A striking fusion of culture and society took place at the same time as the Etruscans were absorbed into the community.

Rome adopted many features of the Etruscan way of life. Etruscan dress, in particular the toga and the short cloak known as the *trabea*, became naturalized at Rome. Many of the insignia of the kings remained as the familiar insignia of Roman magistrates. A painting from Caere shows a man, perhaps a king, sitting on an ivory chair which is an exact prototype of the magisterial throne or *sella curulis*. The most impressive of all the insignia, the *fasces* or axe and bundle of rods which symbolized the power to execute or whip, were traditionally held to come from Etruria, and in particular from the city of Vetulonia. Model *fasces*, perhaps a votive offering or funeral gift, were discovered at Vetulonia in 1898. The Roman consuls, and no doubt before them the kings, were preceded by twelve lictors with such *fasces*. The number is said to derive from the league of twelve Etruscan cities each of whose rulers was attended by a single lictor.

Perhaps the greatest debt to Etruria was the alphabet. The Etruscan alphabet was derived from the Greek, although it is uncertain whether it was adopted as a result of contact with Western Greeks after the foundation of Cumae in the late eighth century or whether, as the ivory tablet inscribed with the Etruscan alphabet including the 'Eastern' Greek letter samech, which was found at Marsiliana d'Albegna, has been taken to show, it was adopted at an early date from the Greeks of the Eastern Mediterranean. There is, however, no doubt that the Latin alphabet was a modification of the Etruscan. The letter-form of the earliest Latin inscription, on a fibula from Praeneste (*Manios med fhefaked Numasioi* – Manios made me for Numasios), proves this abundantly. And the same conclusion is reached by observing that the order of the voiced and unvoiced gutturals C and G in the Latin alphabet differs from that in the Greek and is to be explained by the fact that Etruscan lacked voiced consonants.

Rome of the Tarquins was bilingual. Both Etruscan and Latin writing have been found on vases dating from the sixth century. The Etruscan inscriptions include the words *ni araziia laraniia* on a bowl of about 525 BC and the name *uqno* on a fragment of the same date, recalling, perhaps, Aucno the mythical founder of Mantua. The earliest Latin writing in Rome also comes from a vase of the last quarter of the sixth century (*CIL* 1².717 : the so-called Duenos-vase) and other Latin inscriptions have been found on contemporary pottery in the Regia and the Forum Boarium. The regulations about the cult of Diana may have been written in Etruscan (p. 67), whereas the earliest surviving law inscribed on stone, a cippus from the forum, is in Latin. The interpretation of the cippus is obscure but the inscription itself cannot be much later than 500 BC. As far as can be seen Etruscan and Latin co-existed at Rome; and Etruscan only declined as the power of Etruria itself declined, and Rome found her main contacts to be increasingly with her Latin neighbours and others, Oscans and Umbrians, who shared a linguistic affinity.

In the same way, by studying the lists of magistrates and other prominent figures of the early Republic, one can see what very varied backgrounds the leading citizens came from, and there is very little trace of *ethnic* rivalry between them. It is true that there are occasional monopolies of the consulship (as by the Fabii in the 470s) but these cannot be seen as feuds between families of different origin. There are families whose name and tradition betray them as Sabine – the Valerii, the Claudii, the Aurelii. There are others who claimed an Alban origin : Livy (1.30.2) and Dionysius (3.29.7) give two slightly variant lists but the variations are probably not significant and due either to scribal or prestige causes. The list is the Julii (or Tullii), Servilii, Quinctii (or Quinctilii), Geganii, Curiatii and Cloelii. The names are certainly of Latin rather than Sabine or Etruscan derivation. And then there are a host of families whose names betray them instantly as Etruscan – Aternii, Cominii, Herminii, Volumnii, Licinii, Sicinii, Sempronii, Menenii, Poetelii, Larcii. Other names suggest a less-defined Italic background – Considii, Sergii, Duilii, Oppii, Sulpicii, Cornelii. There will also have been Greek and Car-

thaginian merchants who settled in Rome, adding further
variety to an already cosmopolitan city.

How was this unity created? What was the social organization of Rome? Little, if anything, is known of the pre-
Etruscan stage. From a number of different sources it is
possible to reconstruct what the Romans may have believed
their earliest ('Romulean') organization was, but no weight
can be put on it; three tribes (Varro, *On the Latin Language*
5.55; Dionysius 2.7.2; Propertius 4.1), perhaps known as the
Ramnes, Tities and Luceres, and thirty curiae (*coviria* 'gather-
ing of men') which supplied both a political assembly and the
military forces.

It is possible that the earliest inhabitants of Rome did,
like other Indo-European people (e.g. the Dorians) have an
ancestral system of three tribes, but we have no means of
knowing how later immigrants were integrated into these
tribes. Nor can the names which Varro and others preserve
be correct because they are certainly Etruscan and, in any
case, the earlier historical tradition attributes these names
not to tribes but to cavalry squadrons (see p. 43). Still less
can the existence of a three-tribe system in early Rome be
established along the comparative lines which Dumézil has
elaborated, whereby Indo-European communities are supposed
to have been divided into three groups – priests (Ramnes),
farmers (Tities) and warriors (Luceres).

With the Curiae we are on firmer ground, because features
of their organization survived on into historical times. A Curia
was both a group of people and a building where that group
could meet. Each Roman Curia originally had such a building
but by the late Republic they had been reduced to two in
number – *curiae veteres* and *curiae novae*, four Curiae using
veteres and the remainder *novae* (Festus 180L.). The purpose
of the buildings was to act as a meeting-place for discussion,
for religious ritual and for dinners which continued down to
the time of Augustus (Dionysius 2.23.5). The Curiae were made
up of different clans (*gentes*) and seem to have possessed some
land (Dionysius 2.7.4: one of the curial festivals, the Forna-
calia in February, was concerned with the purification of
land-boundaries). Historically they numbered thirty and claimed
to derive their names from the Sabines raped by Romulus'

men (Cicero, *On the Republic* 2.14; Livy 1.13.6). In fact, however, that myth springs simply from the name of one of the
Curiae – Rapta – and the other surviving six names imply
either a topographical (Veliensis, Foriensis) or a clan (Titia,
Acculeia) origin. What the true basis of the Curiae was is
hard to discover. Our only specific witness, the scholar Laelius
Felix (Aul. Gell. 15.27.5), says that the assembly constituted
from the Curiae was made up of 'kinds of men' (*ex generibus
hominum*). It is, I think, easiest to understand that phrase
to mean ethnic units. The Curiae, in the first instance, were
formed by homogeneous ethnic groups who will have settled
in a particular locality, just as there are the Hungarian, Greek
and Italian quarters in Toronto today. The Tuscus vicus,
'Etruscan street', was an old land-mark of Rome and there are
good grounds archaeologically for believing that the Quirinal
was indeed a Sabine quarter. If that is right the Curiae were
ethnic wards and their assembly (Comitia Curiata) was the
federal assembly of the different wards.

But three tribes and thirty curiae is very schematic, and if
the idea is right that the Curiae arose from successive settlements of groups of people at Rome, one would expect the
number to increase gradually to a final total of thirty. So
Professor R. E. A. Palmer argues in a very controversial book,
maintaining that the final number of thirty curiae was reached
in the fifth century BC. Alternatively it may have been
the original social organization at Rome, artificially devised
by the Etruscans about 580 BC on the model of the curial
systems in the other Italian towns, which was subsequently
superseded two generations later by the centuriate and tribal
reorganization of Servius Tullius.

The Curiae also formed the voting units of a political
assembly which survived in skeleton form throughout the
Republic with thirty lictors representing the thirty Curiae.
There is no doubt that it was the original assembly at Rome,
even if we do not know how many members it had, because
in its most attenuated form in the late Republic it was still
responsible for passing the law that validated every holder of
magisterial power (*imperium*), and so too had presumably
confirmed the appointment of the kings in the Regal period.
It also authorized the transition of a man from one *gens* to

another (Aul. Gell. 15.27) and adjudicated on wills.

The curial system, if it was something along the very bare lines indicated above, had at least three disadvantages for a progressive and expanding city. In the first place, if it was based on wards, it became cumbersome to operate when citizens moved from their original wards. Secondly, although it catered for the large groups of immigrant citizens (whole *gentes* or the like), it was ill-suited for the registration of the individual immigrant. Thirdly, since, according to tradition, it was also the basis for the recruitment of the army (each *curia* being supposed to provide 100 men for the infantry), it was unwieldy and arbitrary, particularly when the need arose for men to be chosen on a uniform and standardized qualification of ability to provide the regulation armour. One corollary therefore of Servius' reform of the army in the period 550-530 BC (see p. 64) was the creation of a new assembly formed of all the centuries of the *classis*, the group of people qualified for cavalry and infantry service. This assembly, the Comitia Centuriata, was the assembly of the soldiers – the *exercitus* – and, as such, it met outside the sacred boundaries of the city (the *pomerium*), because the mobilized army was not allowed inside the city. It was also the assembly of the wealthy upper-middle class, which gave a much greater say to the group which was economically important to Rome. It became, after the fall of the kings, the dominant assembly for both legislative and electoral purposes.

Servius' creation of the *classis* was designed to provide a common and universal method of identifying and classifying Roman citizens, citizens, that is, whose prime loyalty was to Rome and not to family or ethnic group. But in a city as large as Rome, smaller units were also required for administrative purposes. These Servius provided by a reorganization of the tribal system. The facts about it are very difficult to ascertain, particularly since we have no clear idea what it was designed to replace. Basically it is certain that there were four city-tribes (based on hill-names: Palatina, Collina, Esquilina and Sucusana; so Varro, *On the Latin Language* 5.56; Festus 506L.; Pliny, *Natural History* 18.13; Dionysius 4.13) and a number of country-tribes. In historical times there were thirty-one country-tribes which were extended to cover the whole of Italy and beyond, but that total was only reached in 241 BC after the conquest of Italy, and there are records of the creation of fourteen country-tribes between 387 and 241 BC. Under the year 495 BC Livy (2.21.7) notes that thirty-one tribes were made (*una et triginta tribus factae*) but the text is almost certainly corrupt and twenty-one should be read (XXI for XXXI). The easiest explanation is to suppose that two country-tribes, the Claudia and Clustumina, which continued throughout Roman history, were added then to deal with an influx of Claudii (p. 90) and the capture of land up-river from Rome round Crustumerium (p. 91). If so, it could be maintained that Servius instituted four city-tribes and fifteen country-tribes (or sixteen if the Claudii migrated to Rome earlier and only one tribe was added in 495 BC to bring the total up to twenty-one: see p. 91). This has been disputed on the grounds that the names of some of those fifteen tribes (e.g. Romilia, Sergia) are derived from families whose only prominence in history was in the second half of the fifth century. But we do not know enough about how the tribes were named at all to rely on such arguments: the only reasonably secure point is that they do seem to have been named after families.

Secondly, however, other and earlier historians claimed that Servius divided the Roman territory not into four city and fifteen country-tribes, but into four city and either twenty-six or thirty-one country-tribes. There are however good reasons for doubting these alternatives. The one is simply attributing to the original innovator the total *final* number of tribes (thirty-five), whereas the other would seem to be equating Servius' tribes with the thirty traditional Curiae that had preceded them. Neither makes as good historical sense as the view that the tribes increased in number gradually as the Roman world expanded.

The Servian country-tribes took their names from families, perhaps because at some time the families had worked or owned land there. They were territorial regions. Membership of a tribe conferred citizenship; it also conferred obligations – the obligation to pay tribute and the obligation to be assessed for military service. Since it was a territorial registration, it meant that citizenship became dependent no longer on ethnic origin or birth but on residence coupled with some financial qualification – which must have enfranchised a large number of the more recent Etruscan and other immigrant merchants and farmers. Once citizenship had been established, it was no longer necessary to continue to reside within the territorial limits of the tribe to exercise the rights of citizenship, as seems to have been the case with the Curiae. The tribal system made for unification and the breakdown of social and ethnic barriers.

In an emerging community racial factors are often important, but equally are often submerged by new tensions which arise from other conflicts of interest within the society itself. The Servian reforms seem very largely to have succeeded in unifying Rome racially : it became and remained a state in which Etruscan and Latin were naturalized together. But they did not succeed in bridging a much more serious division that was to break out into strife once the restraining hand of the kings had been removed.

The oldest advisory body known at Rome was the Senate – the council of elders. Its members were called the Patres – the fathers, that is, as is generally agreed, the heads of the clans or *gentes*. There are various traditions about its creation and evaluation. The orthodox view was that Romulus chose 100 Patres and that by the early Republic the total had risen to 300 (e.g. Livy 2.1.10), as a result of Sabine, or Alban, and Etruscan additions. (The main variants are given by Dionysius 2.12, 47, 57; Festus 454L.; Plutarch, *Romulus* 13; Livy.) The ultimate number of 300 is undoubtedly connected with a long-standing tradition that originally the Patres were chosen from the Curiae, on the basis, it must be supposed, of ten per Curia, just as under the Empire the members of local municipal Curiae or Senates were still known as *decuriones*. Indeed a Republican act of uncertain date (the plebiscitum Ovinium; after 362 BC) perpetuated the regulation that senators should be chosen from Curiae (*curiatim*: Festus 290L.). If there was a fixed number for the Senate under the Etruscan kings, say 300, then not all the heads of all the main branches of the clans could take their seats and some principle of selection was required, such as nomination by the Curiae or appointment by the king. In consequence the heads of clans who formed the Senate were distinguished from the other heads of families by the fuller title – Patres Conscripti or enrolled Fathers. This, at any rate, seems to me the natural interpretation of that title and is clearly how both Cicero, who speaks of a single senator as *pater conscriptus* (*Philippic* 13-29) and Dionysius, who translates it as *pateres engraphoi* (2.47), interpreted it. But other interpretations are possible, and Momigliano has recently argued at length for the view that Patres Conscripti denotes two separate groups – hereditary Patres and others who, as a result of wealth and success, have been additionally enrolled (i.e. Patres et Conscripti) just as the phrase Populus Romanus Quirites means the Roman People and the Quirites. Such a combination of a hereditary aristocracy and a propertied class neatly reflects the new organization created by Servius Tullius, who for the first time made it easy for the *nouveaux riches* to have a say in the government of Rome. And it has some support in three notices in the lexicon of Festus (Paulus-Festus 6, 36L: Festus 304L.) which speak of the *patres* and the *conscripti* as separate members of the Senate.

For the great social cleavage of the early Republic was a cleavage, according to Livy and all our other sources, between two groups – the Patricians and the Plebeians. What was the ground of this cleavage and who comprised the two groups? The patricians are the easier to define: *patricii* means the sons and descendants of Patres just as aedilicii means the sons and descendants of aediles.

But the facts are more complicated than this. At some stage the patricians were restricted, not to the descendants of *any* Pater, but to a limited number of particular families, classified as greater and lesser families (*maiores* and *minores gentes*). The lesser families were said to have been created by the elder Tarquin (Livy 1.35.6; Cicero, *On the Republic* 2.36; Dionysius 3.41: cf., however, Tacitus, *Annals* 11.25, who attributed them to the early Republic). Unfortunately we do not know which families, apart from the Papirii, comprised the *minores gentes* and so cannot say whether there was any difference in historical or ethnic origin between them and the *maiores*. The one distinguishing quality about all of these families was that they inherited certain special religious privileges. Until the third century BC the three great priests of Jupiter, Mars and Quirinus, the head of the Curiae (*curio maximus*) and the *rex sacrorum* (the priest who inherited the king's religious duties after the fall of the kings) had to be patricians. Above all when the kingship fell vacant, the residuary religious powers of the state, which were the *auspicia* or the power to consult the will of the gods, and so to appoint a successor, reverted to the patricians. A series of patrician 'between-kings' (*interreges*) continued a caretaker government until a new king was agreed. And this continued under the Republic whenever both consulships became vacant through death or invalid election, except that *interreges* had not only to be patricians but also to have held the office of consul themselves.

As for the plebeians, the dichotomy patrician-plebeian might suggest that they were simply the rest of the people, the nonpatricians. However two quite different opinions have been expressed about the real nature of this traditional social division.

1. A. Alföldi, in a series of books and articles, developed a theory that the patricians were to be identified with an aristocracy of knights who formed the royal cavalry, originally 300 and later doubled to 600 and called the Sex Suffragia (see p. 46). This *corps d'élite* assumed power, he believes, on the fall of the kings and maintained themselves a self-perpetuating circle of office-holders. It was this aristocratic monopoly based on the role and importance of a cavalry restricted to patricians that exacerbated relations with the rest of the people – the plebeians. Alföldi bases his story on three main arguments :

a. Festus (290L.) says that in the Servian organization there was a unit called 'procum patricium'. He derived his knowledge of it from Varro, and Cicero (*On the Orator* 156) throws a little more light when he mentions that in the handbooks of the censors, who were responsible for the assessment of the classes and the distribution of the centuries, there was a reference to a *centuria fabrum et procum*. We know from elsewhere of at least one centuria of *fabri* (smiths). So Cicero is probably alluding also to a separate century of *proci* and abbreviating their full name which was *proci patricii*. But neither Cicero nor Varro say whether the century was a cavalry or infantry century and, by implying that there was only a single one, rule out the possibility that it can be the same as the six centuries of cavalry (Sex Suffragia). The most probable interpretation is that it was a century comprised of patricians (sons and descendants of Patres) which voted first in the Assembly (*proci* = *proceres* = leaders) for religious reasons, because a great deal of superstition was attached to the way in which the first century voted.

b.   Patricians in classical times wore a certain sort of shoe which Alföldi thought was essentially a riding-boot. But there is no evidence for the identification.

c.   Alföldi's main argument was an a priori one, that the cavalry must have been the dominant force in the Roman army. But I have argued that this ceased to be true after the mid-sixth century (see p. 43). And the fact that cavalry were provided with a horse and fodder at public expense from earliest known times makes it most unlikely that they were all wealthy aristocrats.

2.   Momigliano effectively refuted Alföldi's case and has advanced one of his own. For him the patricians, strictly so called, are too small a class to be socially divisive in such a large and cosmopolitan community as Rome. They can have been not many more than a mere 1,000, whereas the male population of Rome is not likely to have been less than 30,000 and may have been as high as 80,000 if the earliest census totals recorded in the annalists may be believed. He sees the social division as a different one, between the *populus*, defined as all those whose property or wealth qualifications entitled them to be assessed as part of the *classis*, and the *plebs*, that is the rest who were *infra classem* (below the *classis*). The distinction between *populus* and *plebs* is found in a few texts (Livy 25.12.10; Cicero, *pro Murena* 1) and the dictator was known also as the *magister populi*. It corresponds very neatly with his view that the senate was drawn from the same class of qualified citizens – *patres* and *conscripti*.

Nevertheless, although the real cleavage must have been –

as it always is – between rich and poor, I doubt if Momigliano's theory is right. Nothing can be based on two, even formulaic, references to the *populus* and *plebs*, when the context tells us nothing about what (if any) the distinction was supposed to be. For tradition asserts, without hesitation and without explanation, that the quarrel was between Patres (by which the patricians are meant) and Plebs. A list of patrician families can be compiled by considering who held certain exclusively patrician position in the early Republic (such as that of interrex). It includes the Aemilii, Claudii, Cloelii, Cornelii, Fabii, Furii, Julii, Manlii, Nautii, Papirii, Postumii, Quinctii, Servilii, Sulpicii and Valerii. And others might be added; but it is very difficult to use the evidence of later history, because families die out or split into branches, some of which were recognized as patrician and some not, and individuals could transfer to plebeian status (as P. Clodius did in 59 BC) and thereby alter the status of their descendants in perpetuity. But, at some point, patrician status became restricted, and merely to have been elected a Pater, i.e. a member of the Senate, ceased to entitle your sons to be patricians. When was that? Certainly after the arrival of the Claudii (according to tradition, they came in 504 BC after the fall of the kings (Livy 2.16.4; Dionysius 5.40; Servius, on *Aeneid* 7.706), but they may have arrived somewhat earlier, see p. 91), and before the first recorded civil disturbances with the plebeians in 494 BC. To me the most economical explanation is that patricians ceased to be created as of right when the kings, as dispensers through their sovereign authority of sacral nobility, were finally expelled and replaced by a Republic. Until then all members of the Senate were automatically patricians. The distinction between the two classes of patrician families (*maiores* and *minores gentes*) reflects the historical fact of the dynasty. Such families need not necessarily have been Etruscan influx of new families into the Senate under the Etruscan themselves (the Papirii, for instance, seem to have come from the Alban Hills) but they were embraced into Roman society as part of the great expansion which the Tarquins set in motion.

The patricians, strictly so called, may indeed have been

limited in number, but their power was great. In the first
place, they will have attracted to them many wealthy and
substantial merchants who had not yet become involved
in actual politics or who were not heads of clans. Secondly,
the families which furnished the patrician class were also
the families which are spoken of as fostering an almost feudal
relationship between heads of families and their dependants,
patroni and *clientes*. The *patroni* had various quasi-legal obligations towards their dependants – e.g. to help them at law or
in need – while the *clientes* had services to fulfil towards their
patrons – e.g. personal attendance. The Claudii, we are told,
arrived with a large body of their *clientes*, while the Fabii
garrisoned Cremera with a force drawn from Fabian *clientes*.
In other words patricians could call upon the loyalty of a
substantial body of men who were bound to them by ties of
sentiment and obligation, and who, when times were hard
economically, would look to them for support and assistance.
But thirdly and most importantly, the patricians had religious control of the main areas of government and administration. The Calendar was not yet an openly published document: only the patricians knew on what days legal or political
business could be done. The ordinary artisan or shop-keeper
who got into the courts for debt and did not enjoy the pat-
ronage of a patrician, would thus find himself at a hopeless
disadvantage. When, fifty years later, the Twelve Tables were
published, it was the mere fact that the current law was now
published, openly available, which mattered, and not any
reforms or innovations. It was the plight of such ordinary
citizens, most of them unattached and recent immigrants,
who worked in the city rather than on the land – as potters,
bronze-smiths, traders and the like – which became desperate
when times were hard during the depression of the early
Republic. They had no one to protect them and were hindered
at every turn by the secrecy and scrupulosity of a religious
cabal. The fact that the residuary powers of the state (the
auspicia) rested with the patricians meant in effect that the
patricians enjoyed a power of veto over the decisions of the
Assembly. And long before the last Tarquin was expelled, there
are traces of this patrician pressure-group beginning to exert
its influence (see p. 77).

In short, therefore, I think that towards the end of the Etruscan dynasty at Rome there did arise a division between a hereditary class, which was backed by a large number of dependants and which relied for the perpetuation of the position very much upon its monopoly and manipulation of religion, and a larger group of independent, unprivileged, poorer and vulnerable men.

We can only speculate how far the developments which have been outlined in the previous two chapters were the doing of particular individuals. The Etruscan dynasty at Rome is said to have been founded about 616 BC by a Tarquin from the town of Tarquinii who was the son of a Corinthian Demaratus, a refugee to Etruria. It is hard to know what, if any, truth there is in any of this but it may be that there is a hard core of fact. There were Corinthians who fled to Etruria about 650 BC when the Bacchiad aristocracy was overthrown by the tyrant Cypselus, because there is unmistakable evidence of Corinthian craftsmen working at Falerii and elsewhere after that date. Etruscan influence begins to make itself felt at Rome, through imports and other artefacts, from the last quarter of the seventh century. The name Tarquinius is a Latinized form of a common Etruscan name *tarcna*, which is found, for instance, in a series of remarkable tombs at Caere dating from the fifth to the third centuries. A Roman Tarquin is known independently, from Etruscan sources, by a wall-painting in the François tomb at Vulci, which depicts a hero Cneve Tarkunies Rumach – Cn. Tarquinius the Roman.

But that is almost all that can be said. Nothing can be asserted about the character or the policy of the first Etruscan king, alleged to be L. Tarquinius Priscus. The stories that fill the pages of Livy are either Hellenistic romances or highly generalized memories of Etruscan achievements at Rome during the Regal period.

With Servius Tullius, traditionally the next king and traditionally dated *c.* 578 BC – *c.* 534 BC, the situation is only a little better. His name is at least firmly associated with two things – the Servian Constitution and the Temple of Diana on the Aventine – and there may have been documentary confirmation of both attributions, but there will have been few other written records of his reign. Furthermore, his whole policy has been distorted out of recognition by three facts. First, the appalling tendency of the Romans to seek etymological explanations for anything easily tempted them to see Servius as the friend of slaves (*servi*), and, presumably, to invent a servile origin for him as well. Secondly, Roman historians tended to categorize the kings of Rome, according to various systems going back ultimately to Plato's cyclic theory of history: Numa the Priest King, Romulus the Warrior Founder, Tarquin the Proud Tyrant, and so on. Servius was seen as the Second Founder, the man who established Rome on a basis of law and who, therefore, attracted many constitutional and legal innovations to himself. Thirdly, his interposition between Tarquins led to speculation about his identity. The Emperor Claudius tried to reconcile an Etruscan story about an adventurer called Macstarna (which is an Etruscan form of the Latin *magister* – master), who gained power at Rome, with the apparent usurpation of Servius Tullius by identifying the two characters; but in this he was unique – and wrong. Nevertheless, all three distortions may convey something historical about the man and it may be possible to make some inferences about him.

For a start, the name Servius Tullius, unlike Tarquinius, is uncompromisingly Latin. So too his mother's name, Ocrisia, is derived from an old Italic root *ocri* – meaning a mountain (Festus 192L.; cf. Umbr. *ukar*, Greek *okris*). And the town from which he is said to have emigrated, Corniculum, is a Latin town, probably Mte dell'Incastro, not far from Rome to the east. Nevertheless his rise to power must have been both unpredictable and abrupt, since he had no hereditary claim to the throne which must already have been in Etruscan hands. The Roman historians did their best. The inexplicable could only be explained as divine. Servius' mother was made pregnant by a divine flame (Dionysius 4.2). This, as with many heroes of Roman and other mythology who lacked pedigrees, established his claim to the highest nobility. Servius' mother was captured as a slave (*serva* – Servius) when Tarquin the Elder took Corniculum, but the boy's intelligence and the mother's respectability ensured that he was brought up in the royal palace until his authority was so much respected that he naturally succeeded to the throne on Tarquin's death. In other words, Servius was a Latin and an upstart.

But the distinguishing qualities of his reign were the

acceleration of the fusion of native and Etruscan, which gave Rome its particular stamp and impetus, and the emergence of Rome as a leading power in Latium. No dates can be assigned to the reign beyond the very vague limits of *c.* 550-520, which are based on the probable archaeological date for the introduction of the new hoplite armour for which he was responsible and on the final fall of the kings in *c.* 507 BC (allowing an adequate span for the last Tarquin).

The policy of fusing native and Etruscan will have had a particular appeal for a Latin who could see the advantage that Rome stood to gain by her advance in civilization and prosperity. So Servius reorganized the army, adopting infantry armour and techniques from Etruria which required the service not just of an élite aristocracy, but of all citizens wealthy enough to afford the equipment and the time for training. This innovation in itself was a great leveller (see p. 45). The rich Etruscan merchant and the old-established Latin land-owner alike were united in a common discipline and uniform. But, snce he was creating a citizen-army as opposed to a military élite, he had to ensure that all those who lived and worked in Rome and who shared in the common life of the city, should be equally eligible to serve in the army, if their wealth qualified them. To do so involved changing the basis of citizenship. And this he did by replacing the old curial system under which citizenship depended principally upon ethnic origin, by a tribal system, under which citizenship depended upon residence (p. 54). Most important of all he recognized that his new army, because it was a citizen army, should have some say in decisions affecting the whole state, just as the military reforms at Sparta *c.* 675 BC were attended by changes in the powers of the Spartan Assembly. The *classis* met by centuries as a deliberative Assembly, and therefore, as a potential rival to Curial Assembly. We do not know the size of the original Comitia Centuriata. The most likely estimate is that it contained thirty centuries of *iuniores* (men of military age), thirty of *seniores* and six centuries of cavalry (the Sex Suffragia, who voted *after* the infantry). But this is only based on speculative reconstruction. There may have been as many as forty centuries of *iuniores*. Nor can we tell how powerful it was under the kings. The sources speak of a procedural

1. A Neolithic hut-urn from Strelice, Czechoslovakia
(PHOTO : THE MANSELL COLLECTION)

above: 2. Macstarna frees
Caeles Vibenna. Wall
painting from the François
tomb in Vulci
(PHOTO: PETER CLAYTON)

right: 3. The death of
Tarquinius Superbus. Wall
painting from the François
tomb in Vulci
(PHOTO: PETER CLAYTON)

right: 4. Votive statuette
of Aeneas carrying Anchises
(PHOTO: MUSEO NAZIONALE
DI VILLA GIULIA)

below: 5. Dedication to Castor
and Pollux

6. Detail of the reconstruction of the façade of
the Temple of Jupiter on the Capitol (PHOTO : PETER CLAYTON)

handbook of Servius Tullius which regulated the election of the first consuls (Livy 1.60.4), but this may be no more than another instance of the tendency to attribute everything constitutional to Servius Tullius. If such a handbook had any reality, it would imply that the Comitia Centuriata was envisaged by Servius Tullius as an *elective* body (electing superior officers in the legion for instance) as well as a deliberative one. Whatever its exact role and power, it will once again have served to mix Romans of every background together in joint discussion about their own state.

The temple of Diana was his largest known monument. The temple itself has not been excavated and cannot be reconstructed with any degree of certainty. It was preceded by an altar in a grove (*ILS* 4907). But the fact that it was a temple shows acceptance of Etruscan religious concepts, and its genuineness is strongly confirmed by Dionysius' explicit statement that a bronze inscription survived until his time, which recorded the decisions made by the cities participating in the cult and the names of their cities. This inscription, he says, was written in archaic Greek letters. He may mean Etruscan, although Latin is not inconceivable since Festus quotes the word *nesi* from the terms of the altar of Diana, and it must be presumed that the inscription mentioned Servius Tullius himself (4.26: Tacitus (*Annals* 12.8) records that the Emperor Claudius spoke of rites which should be paid to Diana *ex legibus Tulli regis* – 'according to the laws of King (Servius) Tullius' – which may again imply a written record). The institution of the cult of Diana was one of the most significant moves of international politics in the sixth century, because it was clearly modelled on the federal cult of Artemis (=Diana) at Ephesus, as all the sources agree. In fact Mycale with the temple of Poseidon Heliconius, rather than the Artemision at Ephesus, was the cult-centre of the Ionian league in Asia Minor, but it was the temple of Artemis which captured the popular imagination and continued to do so down to St Paul's day and beyond. The cult itself, and the underlying idea behind it of a cult that would unite a large group of cities into a federal whole, probably came not directly from Asia Minor but from the Greek colony at Marseilles (Massilia), which was refounded *c.* 540 BC.

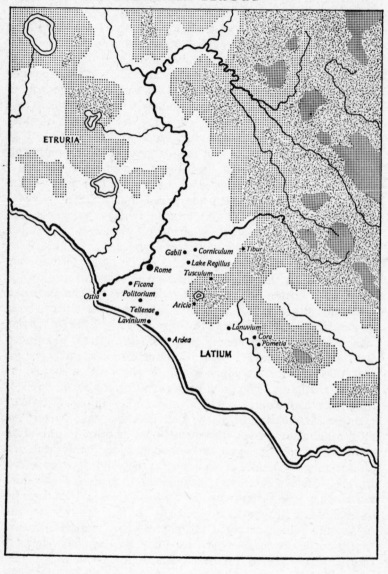

The geographer Strabo (4.180) says that the statue of Diana was set up in the same way as the statue of Artemis at Massilia, which in turn had been derived from Ephesus. The dates suit, and Roman contact with the seafarers of the western Mediterranean is more likely than with the East.

There was, however, a second – and much more obscure – motive behind the cult. Roman historical tradition alleges that there was already in existence a federal cult of Diana in Latium, which brought together a number of different cities for a common purpose. Pliny (*Natural History* 16.242) speaks of an ancient grove of Diana consecrated by Latium on a hill on the outskirts of Tusculum, called Corne. Cato, in a famous fragment of his *Origines* (58 P.) records a dedication in a grove of Aricia made by Egerius Baebius of Tusculum, dictator (or *dicator* – 'dedicator') of the Latins, on behalf of the following peoples jointly: Tusculanus, Aricinus, Lanuvinus, Laurens, Coranus, Tiburtis, Pometinus, Ardeatis Rutulus.

This evidence in itself would be sufficient to prove that Diana acted as the focus of a religio-political league, just as the Ionians were united by a religious league. The difficult question is to decide when the foundation of the Latin league of Diana was. Was it the cause or the consequence of Servius' temple on the Aventine?

1. Momigliano has argued that Servius' temple was the original cult which aimed to unite Latium in a common purpose with Rome. His case rests on the fact that not only Aricia but all Italy recognized a single date (13 August) as the foundation-date of the temple-cult of Diana and that this would only be so if Rome had set the precedent. Besides, some archaeological evidence has come to light about the cult at Aricia. The surviving remains cannot be dated much before c. 500 BC and the cult-statue at Aricia, which took the form of a three-figure Diana and is represented on coins of P. Accoleius Lariscolus in 43 BC, must be even later than that. The cult of Aricia would, in that case, belong to the period of the early Republic when Latium was trying to assert its independence of Rome (see p. 99).

2. Alföldi and R. Schilling accept the priority of the cult of Aricia but date the foundation of the Aventine Diana not to the reign of Servius Tullius but to the 490s, when the

Latin cities, and in particular Tusculum, were conclusively defeated at the Battle of Lake Regillus (see p. 99). Diana changed sides, forsaking Tusculum and Aricia for Rome. They argue that the attribution to Servius Tullius was simply motivated by the fact that slaves (*servi*) had a part in the cult.

3. I have no doubt that the Aventine cult was founded by Servius Tullius about 540 BC. The connection with Marseilles and the express mention of the original terms of the federal cult strongly suggest this. Nevertheless, the traditional account should not be dismissed out of hand. A federal cult in Latium may have existed before 540 BC but, like so many others, with only the barest structure or centre. One further piece of evidence needs to be mentioned. Servius came from Corniculum: there was a Latin cult of Diana at Corne: the foundation legend specified a prophecy that whatever city should be responsible for sacrificing to Diana a certain cow with remarkable horns (*cornua*) would be mistress of the world: it also claimed that the pontifex Cornelius in the end managed to dupe the owner of the cow, a Sabine, into giving Servius the opportunity of sacrificing it. This is a typically frustrating piece of etymologizing which in its latest stage must date from the late third century when Rome was mistress of the world and the family of the Cornelii Scipiones was at its zenith.

However the question of priority between Rome and Aricia be decided, the significant fact is that Servius Tullius instituted a cult whose primary object was to link other Latin cities, through common worship, with Rome. Before this Rome had indeed extended her horizons. A seventh-century expansion to Ostia, at the mouth of the Tiber, to secure the salt trade is entirely credible. The annexation of minor communities in the immediate vicinity of Rome is attributed to the first Tarquin and would be a natural result of the end of Rome's primitive isolation and the beginning of her contact with her Etruscan neighbours. Such activity has received striking archaeological confirmation in recent years. Livy (1.33.1-2) lists Politorium, Tellenae and Ficana as villages captured by the pre-Etruscan king Ancus Marcius. All three lay between Rome and the coast; and Politorium, long identified as Casale di Decima, is now known to have flourished

in the eighth and early seventh century. But the burials in
the cemetery there, discovered in 1953 but only recently
brought to light, stop before 600 BC. This should imply that
the settlement was then abandoned. So now, for the very first
time, a Roman king set out, as a matter of deliberate policy,
to build an alliance. The policy reveals the double strand of
Rome's history – her ties with Latium and her debt to Etruria
which already enjoyed a sophisticated federal system of
Twelve Peoples.

It was the policy of an Etruscanized Latin, as is borne out
by two further points. The temple was built on the Aventine, that is outside the sacred perimeter of the city, a hill
which was only sparsely, if at all, populated at this date
and which only became a residential district after the passing of a bill, traditionally by a tribune of the plebs, L. Icilius,
in 456 BC which released the land for building. Secondly, the
festival of Diana was a holiday for slaves (Plutarch, *Roman
Questions* 100). This is a puzzling fact, quite apart from the
usual fears of etymological fabrication (servi/Servius), because
it is virtually certain that in regal Rome there were no slaves.
They are barely mentioned in the Twelve Tables. The first slave
market was set up in 259 BC and the first plausibly attested
auction of slaves was in c.396 BC after the fall of Veii, when
the size of Rome began to justify slaves as agricultural or
domestic workers. Slaves do indeed figure in the historical
narrative of early Rome but this is no more than a natural
transference from later times. Probably the temple of Diana
was put outside the city to attract not only the formal
allegiance of Latin cities but also the adhesion of dispos-
sessed immigrants, much as Romulus was said to have created
an asylum for runaways. It was only later that this special
concern for the underprivileged came to be specifically confined to slaves. What Servius was concerned to achieve
was the claim of Rome to be the dominant and magnetic
force in Latium and S. Etruria.

The same consistent policy can be inferred from the third
major undertaking connected with his name – the erection of
the twin temples of Fortune and Mater Matuta in the Forum
Boarium, and of the shrine of Fors Fortuna across the Tiber
(Varro, *On the Latin Language* 6.17 : other cults of Fortune

were also periodically referred to Servius but with less circumstantial evidence). There is no archaeological evidence for
Fors Fortuna, but the earliest deposits on the Forum Boarium
site belong to about 560 BC, although the first actual temples
may be as late as 500 BC. Once again we have the pattern
of an open shrine succeeded by a temple. Fors Fortuna
shares some of the same characteristics as Diana. The shrine
was outside the city, and the festival was patronized by slaves
(Ovid, *Fasti* 6.775ff.). Although Fortune was a Latin deity,
we cannot even guess what appeal she must have had for a
king whose whole rise to power may itself have owed a lot
to Fortune. But Fortune in the Forum Boarium was symbolized by a veiled statue (which survived down to the time
of the Emperor Tiberius : Dio. 58.7.2). Such statues – *di involuti*
– recall the veiled statues of Etruscan gods of Fate and
suggest Etruscan influence in the foundation of that cult.
Mater Matuta, on the other hand, is a defiantly Italic/Latin
deity, perhaps of child-birth. The name echoes her Oscan
counterpart – Maatuis – and her principal shrine was at the
Latin town of Satricum. At a late crisis of history, when
Rome was hard-pressed by Veii in 396 BC, Camillus was to
restore the cult of Mater Matuta at Rome in a deliberate
attempt to secure the goodwill of Satricum, one of the key
cities in Volscian territory to the south of Rome. The twin
temples in the Forum Boarium, which also shared a common
birthday (11 June), have been unearthed near the Church
of S. Omobono. They nicely polarize the aim of Servius' policy
– the fusion of Latin and Etruscan.

It was the policy of Greek tyrants, in order to distract attention from their own position as much as anything, to occupy their people with grandiose building programmes and ambitious international adventures. This had been the way of Polycrates of Samos and of Pisistratus at Athens. Something of the same policy can be seen behind those actions which, when once one has stripped away the veils of imaginative romance surrounding his reign, can reasonably be attributed to Tarquinius Superbus.

There is no point speculating whether he was indeed, as Roman legend supposed, the son or grandson of an older Tarquin who had been superseded by Servius Tullius. There is no evidence to control such speculations. Rather, we must be content with the very firm tradition that Tarquinius was the last king of Rome and that he reigned for some years until his expulsion about 507 BC. Quite when he succeeded Servius Tullius cannot be established exactly, but an accession date between 530 and 520 BC would not be unreasonable.

The events of his reign are meagre enough, but they form a consistent picture which continues the broad outlines of expansion initiated by Servius Tullius.

In the first place, he is credited with the construction of the great temple of Jupiter Optimus Maximus; and the fragmentary remains (part of the substructure and antefixes, tiles, etc.) which have been found from the original temple confirm the date, and so the attribution. These remains also enable one to reconstruct its plan and design with a fair degree of confidence, although it had been destroyed by fire in 89 BC and rebuilt in a different style. The original temple was Etruscan in conception, and its sheer size will have been quite awe-inspiring. It was probably 180 feet wide and 210 feet long. It was divided into three chambers, the central one, reserved for Jupiter, being 40 feet wide and the other two 32 feet. The columns supporting the roof must have been over 50 feet high. The entablature and pediment were probably decorated with friezes in relief and sculpture, similar to the fragments found at the Portonaccio temple at Veii. The roof, ornamented with terracotta revetments, was crowned with a huge four-horse chariot (*quadriga*) carrying a statue of Jupiter, holding a sceptre and thunderbolt.

Like the Parthenon at Athens, it proclaimed the power and pride of the city of Rome. It was the largest temple of the time in the whole Etruscan world and it had few rivals even among the Greeks.

Tarquin is also claimed to have built stands in the Circus Maximus for the benefit of spectators (Livy 1.56.2: Dionysius 4.44.1). There is, not unnaturally, no archaeological trace of these; but an early fifth-century tomb at Tarquinii (the Tomb of the Bigae) has a fresco which depicts Etruscan games in full swing – boxers, wrestlers, discus- and javelin-throwing, jumping and dancing, and, above all, horse- and chariot-racing. One notable feature in this picture is the wooden stands for spectators at either side. The games were a great Etruscan delight and it will have been the Tarquins who transplanted them to Rome and who, therefore, may be believed to have equipped the Circus for that purpose. For games serve both for prestige and for popular relaxation. Pisistratus discovered that lesson, when he enlarged and glorified the Panathenaic Games at Athens.

The games at Rome have a complex history which has recently been carefully investigated by Versnel, who gives a lucid and convincing account of the controversy. It is important to distinguish between two sorts of games – the Roman games (*Ludi Romani*) and the votive, or great, games which are first attested for 491 BC and which are only mentioned six times thereafter before 350 BC. The latter were special commemorative celebrations put on to commemorate some great victory or occasion, sometimes in conjunction with a triumph. They need not detain us. The Roman games, however, are more important. They were held annually on 13 September, the birthday of the temple of Jupiter Optimus Maximus, and are explicitly attributed to the Tarquins (Livy 1.35.7; Dionysius 6.95). There is no doubt of their Etruscan origin. The *metae*, the starting and finishing points of the race-course, are depicted on Etruscan monuments; the central

barrier with seven large eggs set up on it, symbolizing the
number of laps, is Etruscan; and the games were preceded by
a procession in which images of the gods (a specifically Etruscan innovation, since they were the first in Italy to have
anthropomorphic representations of gods) were carried through
the streets of Rome to the Circus. There may have been some
earlier indigenous custom, associated with the cult of Consus,
but everything points to the spectacle being introduced by
the last Tarquin as a flamboyant and popular gesture to the
people. Whether it had a particular religious significance, as
Versnel, who sees it as a New Year ceremony, argues, is much
more dubious and much less relevant.

On the international front the evidence is more suspect but,
nevertheless, should not be dismissed out of hand. From early
days, perhaps before 600 BC, Rome had asserted control over
some of the small communities in her vicinity and had begun
to exploit the resources of the saltbeds near the mouth of
the Tiber, which entailed command of the communications
along the south bank of the Tiber. Ostia was traditionally
founded about 625 BC (Livy 1.33.9) and a series of small towns
– Collatia, Corniculum (see p. 63), Ficulea, Cameria, Crustumerium, Ameriola, Medullia and Nomentum, which mainly
lie just north of the Anio – were said to have fallen to the
elder Tarquin (Livy 1.38.4). The exact details are unreliable and
unimportant, but they do indicate something of Rome's sphere
of interest by the mid-sixth century. Servius Tullius extended
it by making a diplomatic bid for the alliance of the Latins
(see p. 68). The annalistic account makes Tarquin act with
greater aggression and lack of scruple. He interrupts a meeting of the Latins at Aricia and, after executing a ringleader,
Turnus Herdonius of Aricia, forces the Latins to sign a treaty
of alliance with himself which gives Rome the predominant
advantage (Livy 1.50-51; Dionysius 4.45). Unfortunately the
details of the story do not bear examination. The name
Turnus Herdonius is an impossible combination and his personality is fabricated from a later Sabine agitator, Appius
Herdonius (Livy 3.15-18: c. 461 BC). The position accorded
to Rome in the treaty is grossly anachronistic. Nevertheless
some conflict with the Latin league of Aricia would in itself
be very probable if we could be sure of the date of the

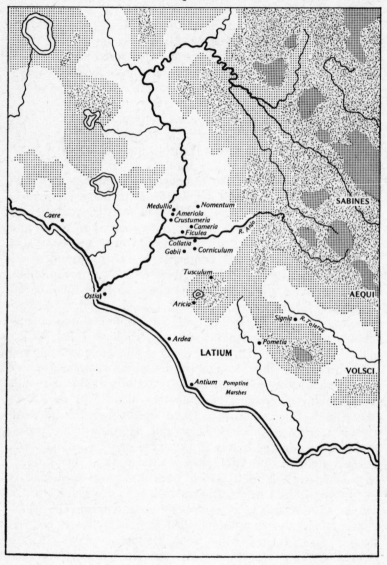

foundation of that league. It is, moreover, relevant to note that Pometia was one of the peoples that figure in the list of dedicators in the grove of Aricia, cited by Cato (fr. 58 P. see p. 67), and is also one of the cities which are explicitly stated to have been captured by Tarquin (Livy 1.53.2), and to have provided spoil worth forty talents of silver which was used for the building of the Capitoline temple. This kind of detail was frequently recorded in dedicatory inscriptions on public buildings, as, for example, L. Plancus in 41 BC set up an inscription commemorating his restoration of the temple of Saturn from spoil, *de manib(is)* (*CIL* 6.1316), and the 'spoils of Pometia' may well have been mentioned in the official inscription in the temple of Jupiter. Pometia lay north of the Pontine marshes, perhaps near the modern Caracupo. Its strategic importance lay in the fact that it was one of the outlying frontier-posts of Latium, bordering on the lands of the Volscians, an Umbrian hill-people, who had by now already begun to press down into the Latin plain and were to threaten Rome's security for much of the fifth century.

Similar considerations apply to Circeii which Tarquin is said to have colonized (Livy 1.56.3). At first sight this seems ridiculous. Circeii is over seventy miles from Rome and the idea of colonization must be anachronistic. Rome was far too small to send out colonies of her own and, in any case, an alternative tradition dating the first Roman colony there to 393 BC (Diodorus 14.102) has positive archaeological confirmation. Yet in the treaty with Carthage concluded or renewed after the expulsion of the Tarquins, which is discussed in detail later, Circeii appears as a comunity in Rome's sphere of influence (Polybius 3.22.11). It again was a frontier site of great strategic importance, as it proved in the fifth century when it passed into Volscian hands.

Together with Signia, a dominant border-site overlooking the River Tolerus and the Via Latina and separating the Volscians from the Aequi, their kindred allies to the north, which Tarquin is also said to have colonized but about which there is no independent evidence, Circeii and Pometia make sense as key-places in a plan to achieve the unity and security of Latium. Tarquin will not have colonized them, but he may have established small allied detachments there from time to time. It is dangerous to exaggerate Rome's supremacy in Latium at this time but the Carthaginian treaty is eloquent testimony that it was not negligible. The treaty is only interested in the coastal dependents of Rome, but the full list – Ardea, which was also one of the Latin states that made a joint dedication at Aricia, like Pometia discussed above and Tusculum which is considered below, Antium, Circeii, Terracina (Anxur) and a corrupt name, possibly the Laurentes (Lavinium) – indicates Roman control over seventy miles of the Latin coast south of Ostia, a formidable but short-lived achievement.

One other expansionist move which can reasonably be attributed to Tarquin was the acquisition of Gabii. It seems to reflect the same policy, for Gabii guards the eastern flank of Latium against the Sabines and is also a jumping-off point for the great corridor between the Apennines and Latium (the Praéneste gap) which links Etruria with Campania. The story of the capture of Gabii as told by the historians (e.g. Livy 1.53-54) is entirely elaborated from two stories in Herodotus and not the slightest credence can be put on it. But Gabii did succumb to Rome, though perhaps not by capture. An ancient leather shield was preserved in the temple of Dius Fidius recording a treaty between Rome and Gabii (Dionysius 4.57.3; Horace, *Epistles* 2.1.24; Festus 48L.). This may date from a subsequent capture of Gabii in the fourth century (discs of this kind were dedicated after the defeat of a city, as after the destruction of Privernum in 329 BC); but it could be genuine as Dionysius asserts. We have seen how such inscriptions *did* survive from the sixth and fifth centuries. But, quite apart from that, Gabii enjoyed a peculiar relationship with Rome which can only be accounted for on the basis of a more or less friendly merger in regal times. Roman officials wore the *cinctus Gabinus* or Gabine dress for certain rituals (Varro, *On the Latin Language* 5.33), and the territory of Gabii had a privileged position in Roman law distinct both from foreign and Roman land.

Moreover Dius Fidius, who was later given a still wider international significance, was a god whose prime function was to watch over the good faith between nations. It is as Dius Fidius that he appears in the Calendars and in the ritual of the Argei. Tarquin is credited with the foundation of his temple – another minor, if suggestive, indication of Tarquin's concern with foreign prestige (Dionysius 9.60.8). Unfortunately no traces of the temple have yet been found to confirm its antiquity. In 466 BC, when Rome was at loggerheads with the Sabines, he assimilated his Sabine counterpart Sancus, presumably in a religious attempt to achieve unity between the two nations; but the attempt failed (see p. 113).

The final piece in this protective ring which Tarquin seems to have aimed at drawing round a united Latium, was the connection with Tusculum, a prosperous city on the rim of the Alban Hills near Frascati. Tusculum was very similar to Rome, a Latin community which, as its very name and its archaeological character reveal, had been heavily Etruscanized during the sixth century. Legend (as perpetuated by Livy 1.49.9) held that Tarquin married his daughter to the chief citizen of Tusculum, Octavius Mamilius, and thereby cemented good relations. The story is not above suspicion. Seventy-five years later, a more historical Mamilius, 'dictator' of Tusculum, earned the gratitude of Rome for anticipating a slave-revolt (Livy 3.18.2), and was rewarded with the gift of citizenship (3.29.6). The two stories look like reduplications of the same event. Here again, however, there is a little more to be said. Tusculum, in common with Ardea (which was in the Roman sphere by the time of the Carthaginian treaty) and Pometia (which was certainly overwhelmed by Tarquin), was a joint-dedicator at Aricia. Indeed the Tusculan people are named first in that list and the dedication was made on behalf of them all by a Tusculan, Egerius (Cato, fr. 58P.; cf. Livy 1.34.3). That is to say, Tusculum was very much one of those Latin comunities which at some stage fell under the sway of Tarquinian Rome. Secondly, the connection between the two communities seems established by the presence in Rome of a *turris Mamilia* of great antiquity. It figures in the ancient, perhaps even pre-Etruscan, ritual of the October horse. On the Ides of October a horse was sacrificed to Mars. Its tail (or genitals) was cut off and carried to the Regia: its head was fought over by the residents of the Via Sacra and the Subura. If the Suburans won, they nailed it to the Mamilian tower. Neither of these facts proves the alliance between

Tarquin and Tusculum but in the general international context they do, I think, help to make it less implausible.

Pometia, Circeii, Signia, Gabii, Tusculum – these form the ring drawn round Latium. It is a coherent and comprehensible policy. If it was in fact Tarquin's policy, it is no more than a logical extension of what Servius Tullius had started and it is a policy in keeping with the magnificent scale of Tarquin's architecture.

One last detail calls for investigation. A weird story was passed down that Tarquin sent a delegation to consult the oracle at Delphi as a result of the apparition of a snake in the Regia (Livy 1.56). To be known at Delphi and to know Delphi was the final hall-mark of a Greek tyrant's acceptability and perhaps it is too much to expect there to be any truth in this story which, with its ambiguous response 'whoever kisses his mother (i.e. the earth) will have supreme power at Rome' and the involvement of a dubiously historical figure, L. Junius Brutus, has all the signs of folk-tale. But a connection between Rome and Delphi under Tarquin (not necessarily *this* connection) should not be dismissed out of hand. Rome's neighbour, Caere, had a treasury at Delphi, and her citizens sent a penitential embassy to Delphi after the Battle of Alalia in the 530s (Herodotus 1.167). All Tarquin's actions make him out as a man who had wide horizons and who understood something of the secret and success of tyranny. Contact with Delphi would not have been beyond his means or his imagination.

The Rape of Lucretia is pure melodrama – and the hypothetical speculations of more recent scholars about it are no less melodramatic. But at some point the Etruscan kings gave way to a republican government and that point was one of the most momentous in history.

The traditional story has the virtue of simplicity. One of Tarquin's sons forcibly seduced Lucretia, the wife of his kins-man Conlatinus. Lucretia told what had happened to Conlatinus and her father, Sp. Lucretius, and his friends P. Valerius and L. Junius Brutus. She then committed suicide. Brutus inspired the others to avenge her death and drove the Tarquins from Rome (Livy 1.57.59). By the late Republic the date of this sensational incident had been fixed to the equivalent of 510 BC. This was achieved in two ways. National dates were established for the foundation of Rome and the duration of the monarchy: these were correlated with Greek Olympiad dates. At the other end there was a long list of republican magistrates (consuls and, before them, praetors) who gave their names to the year. This list, the Fasti, extended back in a virtually uninterrupted sequence until the institution of the Republic.

It is here that the difficulties begin. Inevitably there are some gaps in the sequence of magistrates. In particular in the fourth century there are four years which lack eponymous magistrates and were recorded as years in which only a dictator held office. The authorities disagree about these years to such an extent that it may well be true that they were inserted in order to make mathematical sense of a confused chronology. There are, however, two much more serious objections to the early lists.

1. The lists of eponymous magistrates between 510 and 450 BC contain a number of names of people whose families are known in historical times to have been plebeian, and not patrician. Such are the Sempronii, Junii, Minucii, Sicinii, Aquillii, Cassii, and also the Tullii, Sulpicii and Volumnii.

This phenomenon raises three questions. Was the chief magistracy of early Rome confined to patricians? Did those families, which were later plebeian, have patrician branches in early times? Are the lists of eponymous magistrates of the early Republic reliable anyway? These are difficult questions. Recently the tendency has been for scholars, particularly on the continent, to answer 'No' to the third question and, therefore, to eliminate any possible 'plebeian' names from the Fasti (or list of magistrates). This has been done from an essentially a priori starting-point, that the beginning of the Republic must coincide with a break in contact with Etruria. Archaeologically such a break is not discernible until the period 470-450 BC. But it must be said that the break is much more likely to be due to economic reasons (the general decline of Etruria) than to any internal, political cause, since, as we have seen, Rome had become such an integrated Latin-Etruscan community that no purely administrative revolution would dissolve its cultural links. Professor Werner, therefore, and Professor Bloch would date the fall of the monarchy to about 471 BC; Professor Gjerstad even later, to about 450 BC; and even Professor Alföldi would push it down towards 500 BC.

Such an approach is, however, methodologically unsound. We have already seen how much was preserved in the way of inscriptional evidence, and the annual record of the *pontifices* is an obvious medium for the survival of the names of Rome's eponymous magistrates (see p. 17). It is the other two questions which require thorough-going analysis. Now it is an indisputable fact that in 367 BC a law was passed which enabled one of the two consuls each year to be a plebeian (Livy 6.42.9.). The obvious assumption is that before that date both consuls had to be patrician; and this is a reasonable assumption given the exclusive religious powers which were needed by the representative heads of state and which, as we have seen, were the prerogative of the patricians (see p. 60). There is, in fact, no serious difficulty in believing that all these dubious names of the early Republic were genuinely patrician. Many *gentes* had both patrician and plebeian branches. In many families (e.g. the Junii, Tullii and Cassii) there was an enormous gap between the early Republican 'consuls' and the next possessors of that name to hold high office: there need be no direct, lineal connection. Roman law also provided for people to renounce their patrician status in perpetuity, and we know that some (e.g. P. Clodius) did so.

To assume that all the names of the early Fasti were authentic and patrician would be a tidy solution. I think that it may be right. My only reservation is that the early years of the Republic seem to be fluid socially and that attitudes only hardened around 450 BC when, for instance, one enactment of the Twelve Tables, the Decemviral legislation, was that a plebeian should not marry a patrician (Cicero, *On the Republic* 2.63). This law may only have enshrined what was already binding convention, but, equally, it may reflect a polarization between social groups which had intensified during the early Republic. This will only become clear when the circumstances of the Decemvirate are considered.

2. The second problem is more subtle. Many episodes of Roman history have been invented (or at the least distorted) in order to provide Roman equivalents to Greek historical events. The obvious example is the 300 Fabii at Cremera who re-enact the 300 Spartans at Thermopylae. The analogy between the Tarquins and the Pisistratids at Athens has already been alluded to, and the possible synchronism of their expulsion was noticed by at least one Roman scholar, Aulus Gellius (17.21.4). Hippias, the Pisistratid tyrant, was expelled in 510 BC as a result of an abortive (homosexual) love-affair. Tarquin, more characteristically Roman, was expelled as the indirect result of another (heterosexual) love-affair. There may be *some* truth in the oral tradition, but the tendency to assimilate the events to the sad end of Hippias, in date and detail, is unmistakable. As a result 510 BC becomes a peculiarly suspect date.

There are, however, three other facts which are relevant to any attempt to reach a decision about the transition between monarchy and Republic.

The first is an assertion in the Greek historian Polybius (c. 150 BC) that the Romans concluded a treaty with the Car-

thaginians in the first year of the Republic (3.22.4-13) which
he dates by Greek parallels to 508-7 BC. Polybius quotes the
text of the treaty which runs as follows :

A treaty of friendship should exist between the Romans
and their allies and the Carthaginians and their allies on
the following terms :
A.   (1) The Romans and their allies shall not sail beyond
the Fair Promontory, unless driven by weather or enemy
action. Anyone who is forced beyond the Promontory shall
not be allowed to do business there or to acquire anything except what he needs for re-fitting his ship or for
religious purposes. He shall leave within five days.
(2) (Certain trading provisions).
B.   (1) The Carthaginians shall do no harm to the
people of Ardea, Antium, [Areninum], Circeii, Terracina or
to any other Latin people who are subject to the Romans.
(2) The Carthaginians shall keep away from any
cities that are not subject to Rome. If they do capture any,
they shall hand it over unscathed to the Romans. They
shall not install any garrison in Latium. If they do attack
any place, they shall not quarter over-night there.

The treaty is dated in the consulship of L. Junius Brutus and
M. Horatius, the first consuls established after the dissolution
of the monarchy, and this date is associated with the dedication of the Capitoline temple.

No ancient text has been so hotly disputed as this, but the
issues are relatively simple. 1. Do the reported terms of the
treaty make historical sense? 2. Is the mention of Brutus and
Horatius historically credible?

1.   Contact between Carthage and Etruria (and Rome was,
after all, a leading Etruscan town) are well established in the
sixth century. Aristotle knew of an Etruscan-Carthaginian
treaty (*Politics* 1280 a 35) and an Etruscan inscription of the
sixth century has been found at Carthage. This association
was tried in battle at Alalia (*c.* 535 BC) when the Etruscan
and Carthaginian navies fought a bitter battle against the
Phocaeans (Herodotus 1.163). It received sensational confirmation in 1957 when three sheets of gold-leaf, one in Phoenician

and the others in Etruscan, were discovered at Pyrgi, one of the ports of the town of Caere. The texts are not identical but all refer to the dedication of a temple. The Phoenician reads: 'To the Lady Astarte. This is the sacred place made and given by Thefaria Velianas, King over Caere, in the month of the Sacrifice of the Sun as a gift . . . because Astarte has chosen by means of him in the three years of his reign'. The texts cannot be dated precisely on internal grounds but there can be no serious doubt that they belong close to 500 BC. Equally it is not yet absolutely clear what Phoenicians (whether from Carthage or the East) were involved. But the over-riding significance is the contact between the Etruscan and Phoenician-Carthaginian world which is presumed by Polybius' treaty. Such a treaty makes admirable sense in that context.

2. The second objection is more technical. Polybius does not specifically quote the names of Brutus and Horatius within the terms of the actual treaty. Besides there are good grounds for believing that the officials deputed in very early Roman times to negotiate treaties were not the kings or chief magistrates (as the case may be), but special commissioners – *fetiales* (cf. Livy 1.24) – and that it would be their names that were recorded in any formal treaty. But we do not know what kind of document Polybius had access to. Was it the actual treaty? Was it a draft preserved in the archives of the Senate? We are not well enough informed to be able to reject the straightforward (and somewhat surprising) testimony which Polybius advances. He must have had good grounds for naming Brutus and Horatius as the first Republican magistrates and for dating that treaty in 508-7 BC. For all our hindsight, we have no better grounds for rejecting Polybius than we have for accepting him.

But further scruples have been caused by the person of L. Junius Brutus. The family does not occur again until much later when it is plebeian and there was a strong tendency for Roman families to invent celebrated ancestors to shed lustre on their descent. Cornelius and the temple of Diana is a case in point (see p. 68), and Livy complains that the historian C. Licinius Macer arrogated too much too brazenly for the Licinii. Yet it clearly was a strongly held belief among the Junii; for M. Junius Brutus, who played a key role in the assassination of Julius Caesar, exploited the hereditary tradition of opposition to tyrants, just as Livy's account of the expulsion of the Tarquins has overtones of the events of 44 BC. On the other hand, the story which is told of his authorizing the death of his own sons for conspiring the return of the Tarquins is obviously made up and explains the gap between himself and the later generations of Bruti.

The second factor is the date of the dedication of the Capitoline temple. It clearly belongs to the last quarter of the sixth century and it is aggressively Etruscan in design. Every indication of motive and time points to it as being a showpiece dreamed up by an ambitious Tarquin. But the tradition is unanimous that it was actually dedicated in the first year of the Republic by the consul Horatius (Livy 8.7). Now this, as has already been suggested could have been commemorated on a dedicatory inscription. There is, however, a piece of quite extraneous information which has a startling relevance. Livy records (7.3.5-9) that there was an ancient law, written in archaic letters and words, that 'the *praetor maximus* (the supreme praetor) should knock in a nail on the Ides of September (the dedication-date of the Capitoline temple) . . . They say that that nail marked the number of the years, because nailing was unusual at that time . . . A similar custom existed at the temple of the Etruscan goddess Nortia in (the Etruscan town of) Volsinii. M. Horatius, consul, dedicated the temple of Jupiter Optimus Maximus in the year after the expulsion of the kings, in accordance with that law.' The annual ceremony of driving a nail into the wall had, no doubt, an apotropaic intention: it was designed to ward off plagues and diseases. We hear of dictators appointed in later times for the purpose of 'fixing the nail (*clavi figendi causa*: 363, 331, 313, 263 BC). But if it was in origin an annual ceremony, then it could have provided the raw materials for some very accurate chronological research. In 304 BC an aedile, Cn. Flavius, who showed considerable interest in discovering the unpublished secrets of entrenched government, dedicated a shrine of Concordia and explicitly dated it '204 years after the dedication of the Capitoline temple', (Pliny, *Natural History* 33.19). We do not know for certain what led him to such precise calculations; but the nails, if they existed, would have afforded far and away the most convenient basis of computation.

In short there is a strong tradition, perhaps based on an actual inscription, that the temple was dedicated in the first year of the Republic; and this tradition is confirmed in a roundabout way by a calculation which fixes the date of the dedication to 508-7, presumably (since the Ides of September was the temple's 'birthday'), 13 September 507 BC.

The third factor does not give such a precise clue but is relevant all the same. The Regia or Royal House was constructed on a strange plan which was preserved through successive restorations down to late antiquity. It was a temple and not a dwelling-house. It consisted of a trapeziform courtyard on the north side and an oblong building adjoining the courtyard to the south which contained three rooms – a room with a raised circular hearth (the sacrarium Martis), a vestibule, and a small chamber (the sacrarium Opis Consivae). This Regia, which replaced an earlier shrine, can be securely dated to the last decade of the sixth century on the basis of fragments of wall-plaster and imported Greek vases. The significance of this should not be overlooked. When the Tarquins were expelled, some of the religious functions of the king were taken over by a newly created official – the Priest-King (Rex Sacrorum). The Regia was constructed for the performance of certain religious rites and not for the residence of a king; in other words, it was constructed for the Rex Sacrorum, not the Rex. Its date goes far towards confirming the traditional date for the institution of the Republic.

Certainty is unobtainable, but 507 BC is as plausible as any date for the expulsion of the Tarquins. It was put back to 510 BC (with consequent dislocation of the chronology of later centuries, as is seen in the dictator-years or in the fact that the capture of Rome by Gauls, which was conventionally put in 390 BC, can be shown from Greek sources to have occurred in 386 BC) in order to complete the parallelism with the expulsion of the Pisistratids. For convenience I retain the conventional dates for the events of the early Republic but it should be borne in mind that they are likely to be three to four years out in absolute terms.

What followed the departure of the Tarquins is much more obscure. Latin writers assumed an immediate and smooth switch-over to the dual consulship and a more-or-less uninterrupted advance by Rome. In fact it is more probable that there were some years of chaos and that Rome suffered a severe setback which persisted for over half a century. There are a number of conflicting legends and facts surrounding these years, which will have to be considered individually.

1. The ancient law, quoted above, specified that whoever was *praetor maximus* should be responsible for affixing the nail. Although we conventionally use the title 'consul' for the supreme magistrates at Rome, that name, in fact, was not instituted until the Decemvirate at the earliest and, as the encyclopaedist Festus records (249L.), the original name was 'praetor'. It was only when government became more complex that it was found necessary to augment the chief magistracies by establishing the three grades – consul, praetor, quaestor. The title *praetor maximus* (which is also preserved by the same Festus, 152L.) is an oddity. The Roman legal fiction was that the two supreme magistrates had always enjoyed equal authority, but *maximus* implies that one praetor had supreme authority and such a system has analogies both in zilaθ or magistrate (cf. on Porsenna below) of a number of zilaθs, and in Campania, where the *meddix tuticus* of Capua Etruria where the zilaθ purene is taken to mean the leading is defined by Livy (26.6.13) as the supreme magistrate among the Campanians, although other *meddices* are known. It could, therefore, be, as Hanell and others have argued, that there was originally one supreme, eponymous magistrate at Rome. Hanell, indeed, used this hypothesis to exclude the 'plebeian' names in the Fasti and to produce a list of one eponymous magistrate a year for the early period of the Republic; but this, as we have seen, is unnecessary, and there is no reason to suppose that, if there was a *praetor maximus* with one or more subordinates, such a system lasted for more than the year or two of the troubles. The principle of inequality did

however survive in the emergency powers given in time of crisis to a dictator (or Master of the People, *magister populi*, as he was also known; Festus 216L.) with his subordinate Master of Horse, *magister equitum*. The dictatorship is first attested for 501 BC (Livy 2.18.3) but it may well be that during those first six years after the fall of the Tarquins there were changes and experiments in the precise form of government which we cannot now recover.

2. It is against this background that the strange figure of Macstarna should be seen. There are essentially four connected but separate pieces of evidence.

a. The Augustan scholar, Verrius Flaccus, wrote about him but only a mutilated fragment survives (Festus 486L). 'The brothers Caeles and Aulus Vibenna, from Vulci, [came] to Rome [to see or to help] Tarquin with Max [tarna].'

b. The emperor Claudius, in a speech which survives in a copy on bronze from Lyons, mentioned Etruscan historians who said that Servius Tullius had been a constant companion of Caelius Vibenna in all his adventures in Etruria, but Caelius was defeated and Servius with the remnants of Caelius' army had to flee to Rome where he named the Caelian hill after his friend and reigned over Rome as Servius Tullius: 'for in Etruscan he was called Macstarna'.

c. At Vulci itself, a famous wall-painting from the François tomb supplies further details (Plate 10). Caile Vipinas (Caelius Vibenna) is being freed from chains by Macstarna. Professor Heurgon describes the rest of the scene thus:

> Beside them several warrior couples are still fighting and their names are inscribed above each figure: Larth Ulthes is slaying Laris Papathnos Velznach (Lars Papatius of Volsinii); Rasce is slaughtering Pesna Aremsnas Sveamach; Avle Vivines (Aulus Vibenna) is killing an adversary whose name Venthical . . . plsachs is mutilated but suggests a man from Falerii. Last and not least Marca Camitlnas is running his sword through Cn. Tarquinius of Rome. We notice that only the vanquished carry any identification of country. Caelius and Aulus Vibenna, Macstarna, Lars Voltius, Rascius and M. Camitilius did not need, at Vulci, to have their origins clearly stated.

d. A little more is known about the Vibennae. Roman tradition held that they had obtained the right to settle on the 'Caelian' hill as a result of assistance which they had given to Tarquin (or, as a later development of the story held, Romulus). The name Avile Vipiienes appears on a votive inscription on a cup at Veii about 550 BC, and the same name, Avles Vpinas, appears on a red-figure vase apparently painted at Vulci about 450 BC.

What is to be made of all this? The general consensus is that Macstarna and the Vibennae represent swash-buckling condottieri in the early sixth century who may have had some brief contact with Rome. My own feeling, however, is that the intervention of Macstarna and the Vibennae should be located in the chaos following the fall of the Tarquins. Macstarna is the Etruscan form of *magister* (cf. Porsenna below): it is a name based upon a title – *magister populi*. It looks like the deed of an Etruscan adventurer from Vulci seizing the supreme magistracy at Rome with the help of his friends – and eliminating a Tarquin in the process – just as Porsenna from Clusium succeeded for a brief time in establishing his will over Rome. It was a short-lived adventure – and too discreditable to leave a permanent mark in Roman history.

3. If Macstarna is highly disputable, the facts about Porsenna are relatively secure. His name may be a true proper name or it may be formed from the title of the supreme office – zilao purone which in its turn seems connected with the Greek *prytaneus*, 'president'. But Lars Porsenna has an established place in history as ruler of the inland Etruscan town of Clusium who conducted a military foray in strength against Latium with, presumably, Campania as its ultimate objective, where there were already considerable Etruscan settlements in close contact with the Greeks and with an outlet to Greek trade. Porsenna's motives are unknown. At a somewhat later date the Gauls began to exert pressure on the northern areas of Etruria, but this is hardly likely to have become significant until after 500 BC. The first certain Celtic tombs in the Po valley belong to the La Tène epoch. Therefore Porsenna's actions can hardly be interpreted as being due to a desire to escape from Celtic pressure and to create

a new empire for himself. Rather, I think, it has to be understood in a more general context of movements of peoples at the end of the sixth century. The activities of the Aequi and Volscians have already been remarked, and similar restlessness was shown by the Sabines and Hernici. The stability of central Italy was disturbed and before long the corridor between Etruria and Campania was to be severed. It was a time when people were on the march and old solidarities were in disarray. Something of this kind must have been happening at Vulci: at a later date a very similar phenomenon occurred at Veii. It must be significant that the large and prosperous Etruscan settlement at San Giovenale, near Viterbo, comes to an abrupt end about 500 BC. Porsenna's thrust brought him to Rome about 507-6 BC. The orthodox story re-told by Roman historians was that Rome gallantly held out against him, saved by the heroism of Horatius Cocles, Mucius Scaevola and Cloelia. Those stories are, however, the merest folk-tale. The truth which was preserved by Tacitus (*Hist.* 3.72.1) and the elder Pliny (*Natural History* 34.139), was that Porsenna captured Rome and, no doubt, set up a puppet government. For Rome was essentially defenceless against the concerted attack which such a major Etruscan army could mount.

Legend did indeed maintain that Servius Tullius had constructed the first defensive wall round Rome, but the archaeological evidence firmly rebuts this. The first earthen defence-work (*agger*) is reliably dated by a small fragment of pottery to about 475 BC.

Legend also tried to encourage the belief that Porsenna was motivated by a desire to restore Tarquin to the throne – one Etruscan helping another – but there are no good grounds for supposing that a king of Clusium had any affection for or interest in a Tarquin. The idea is, in fact, ruled out by Porsenna's subsequent fate. Not long after the conquest of Rome, he delegated his military enterprise to his son Arruns who penetrated further into Latium but was met near Aricia by a coalition of Latins and Greeks from Cumae under the command of Aristodemus. Arruns was decisively defeated, and Rome was enabled to resume her independence. The battle of Aricia is recounted at length by Dionysius of

Halicarnassus in a way which suggests that he is drawing on non-Roman sources (it has been argued that there was a local history of Cumae) and which, therefore, can be regarded as giving an independent, non-Roman light on events. Tarquin, again, does not seem relevant to this encounter. After his expulsion he was discredited. He is alleged to have spent some time at Caere and at Tusculum, and to have died as Aristodemus' guest at Cumae. Porsenna and Aristodemus cannot both have wanted to restore him : it is unlikely that either did.

But Porsenna's inroads, quite apart from the disturbance that they must have caused to internal Roman politics, contributed to the break-up of the unified Latium which had existed at the end of Tarquin's reign. The whole area had become fragmented once more. No longer could Rome claim that from the mouth of the Tiber to Anxur (Tarracina) and from Gabii to Pometia was 'subject' to her. Each small community was left to fend for itself.

4. It is against that background that one of the more unexpected curiosities of Roman history needs to be viewed. The annalistic historians recalled that in 505 BC a distinguished Sabine, Attus Clausus, with 5,000 of his dependants migrated to Rome and settled on the outskirts of the town (Livy 2.16.4; Dionysius 5.40; Plutarch, *Publicola* 21). This was not the only account of how the Claudii reached Rome. Suetonius, deriving his information from the circle of the Claudian emperors, affirmed that this migration was as remote as the time of Romulus, whereas Appian, drawing on older sources but writing about AD 150 (*Reg.* 12), dated it to the time of the Tarquins. It is very difficult to establish anything conclusive in a dispute of this kind. Essentially there are two incompatible approaches to the problem.

a. The Claudii were certainly a patrician family and furthermore they had a special burial ground of their own beneath the Capitol (Suetonius, *Tiberius* 1). These two facts indicate that the family enjoyed a very privileged position, and it is hard to see how they could have been classed as patrician unless they had received that status from a king, presumably an Etruscan king. On that argument, their migration should have occurred before 507 BC.

b. On the other hand, it is attested that the number of tribes was increased to twenty-one in 495 BC – and it is assumed that this was by the creation of the Claudia and the Clustumina (incorporating the territory of Crustumerium captured in 499 BC). It is difficult to account for the Claudia except on the basis that it comprised the land settled recently by the Claudii (Livy 2.21.7).

In the face of this conflict judgement must be cautious. It could be argued that the Claudii post-dated their arrival deliberately, for propaganda reasons, so that they should be thought to be the great upholders of liberty, unsullied by any contact with the monarchy. It could equally be argued that they projected their arrival back to Romulus or Tarquin in order to secure the respectability of a continuous pedigree. On the whole, I am inclined to accept the annalistic date because it fits the disturbed conditions of the time when large bodies of people were on the move and when the constitutional position was still, for a year or two, in such uncertainty that it was possible to establish patrician status as the *pater* of a family, represented in the Senate. But it would not affect the over-all picture if the Claudii in fact had become naturalized any time between 550 and 507 BC. Indeed it may be the case that only one tribe (the Clustumina) was created in 495 BC and that the number had previously been twenty. The sources do not formally say that two tribes were added but only that the total became twenty-one and there is no a priori reason why there need have been an odd number of tribes at all times, at least until the tribal assembly became a powerful voting body. If so, the Claudii and the Claudian tribe could belong to the mid-sixth century.

Rome now found herself threatened on every side. The annalistic record contains disjointed notices about wars and sudden alarms which, even if they cannot always be accepted in their entirety, give a credible picture of the perilous and fluid situation existing in Latium after the collapse of the hegemony of the Tarquins. Significantly the only people who do not seem to have threatened Rome were her Etruscan neighbours – Veii, Caere and others – which suggests that the Etruscan character of Rome was not in any way affected by the change in regime. But to the south and east vigilant defence was required.

The first front was against the Sabines, the hill-people who lived on the forward slopes of the Apennines with centres at Cures and Reate. Latium offered a standing attraction to the Sabines with its superior pasture and access to the sea. Dionysius of Halicarnassus records four wars against the Sabines in the years 505-500 BC but, although they are dignified with 'triumphs' and victories, they were probably no more than punitive skirmishes. The relevant fact is the existence of Sabine pressure on Rome at this time, which may have inspired the traditional date for the reception and absorption of the Claudii (see p. 91). Livy's account (2.16-18) is partly based upon the same source as Dionysius; but halfway through he switches to a new source, and this involves him in some chronological and historical confusion. For, as a result of using two sources, he reports the same events, namely the affairs of Cora and Pometia, twice under two different years (503 BC and 495 BC: 2.16.8 and 2.22.2) and omits two of the Sabine campaigns recorded by Dionysius in the process. Livy's mistake can however he easily discounted, and the reality of the Sabine threat can be confirmed from an additional incident.

Under 499 BC Livy records the siege of Fidenae, an Etruscan enclave on the left bank of the Tiber north of Rome, and the capture of Crustumeria, the modern Casale Marcigliana,

LATIUM AGAINST THE SABINES AND THE VOLSCI

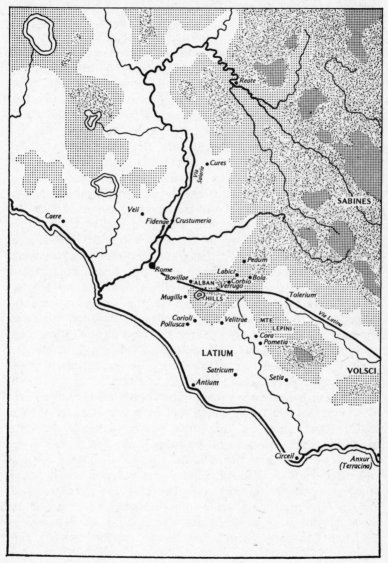

a strategic site dominating both the Via Salaria and an important crossing of the River Tiber. Now neither event is absolutely secure. Dionysius, for instance, gives a rival version that Fidenae was actually captured in 504 BC and that Crustumeria was incorporated as long ago as the reign of Tarquin the Elder (3.49.6). But the Crustumina tribe was created in 495 BC and it is a priori likely that the creation of that tribe followed shortly upon the annexation of the *ager* Crustuminus. If so, the Roman actions with respect to Fidenae and Crustumeria reveal a determined attempt to safeguard the Via Salaria (which afforded the Sabines the most direct access to Rome) and to push the Roman frontier back towards Sabine land and away from the environs of Rome.

The second threat was to the south. Here again it was a case of hill-people – the Volscians – casting covetous eyes on the Latin *campagna*. They had been held at bay for a while by the ambitious strategy of Tarquin, but with the collapse of his power the alliance disintegrated and the Volscians were free to penetrate as and where they could. Their progress can be attested archaeologically as well as by fact and legend. Thus Tarracina, which had been in the Roman sphere of influence at the end of Tarquin's reign, fell to them and was renamed Anxur – a name which survived in the local cult of Jupiter A(n)xoranus (*CIL* 10.6483). Volscian remains are plentiful there from the fifth century. Its neighbour, Circeii, suffered an identical fate; Livy (6.12.6, 13.8, 17.7) speaks of its Volscian sympathies even in the fourth century. Velitrae, like Rome a Latin town which had been Etruscanized (hence its Etruscan name – cf. Volaterra), is mentioned as changing hands on several occasions (see below), as was all too often the fate of a border town, but its Volscian character became well-established in the fifth century and it is the home of the primary evidence for the Volscian language, the so-called Tabula Veliterna (*c.* 350 BC), a long dedication to a local deity called Declun – . Volscian traces have also been detected at Cora and Carascupo (which may be the ancient Pometia), and above all at Antium.

Given this solid archaeological background for Volscian encroachment, one can approach the historical evidence with more confidence. It amounts in essence to an almost annual record of wars or rumours of war, faithfully reported by Livy, over the greater part of the fifth century. But when these are analysed in detail they suggest that the main threat belonged to the first quarter of the century when the Volscians made serious inroads in Latium and threatened Rome itself. There are basically three stages.

1. By 495 the Volscians seem to have established themselved at Cora and Pometia (so Livy 2.22.2, who reports that they agreed as a result of a temporary setback to give hostages from those towns to the Romans). It is not known how or when they acquired them from the Latins (see p. 15), but this loss agrees with a notice in Livy (2.31.3) that in 494 BC the Romans defeated the Volscians near Velitrae (=Velletri) and attempted (abortively) to recolonize it. In other words, by the 490s the Volscians had succeeded in forcing the gap between the Alban Hills and Mte Lepini and so opening up a direct approach to Antium, which also had figured as a Roman dependency in the Carthaginian treaty, but which is next heard of (in 493 BC) as in the hands of the Volscians (Livy 2.33.4). The literary and archaeological evidence is coherent and plausible.

2. The most dramatic episode was the story of Coriolanus. A young soldier, Cn. Marcius, was responsible for the Roman capture of the town of Corioli, as a result of which he acquired the surname Coriolanus. Slighted in his ambitions by his compatriots, he deserted to the enemy, the Volscians, and became their commander, leading them in two attacks up to the very walls of Rome. Only the emotional intervention of his mother deterred him from storming the city. It is impossible to disentangle truth from fiction in this legend, which was in origin a timeless one, not pinned down to any particular date, since Cn. Marcius Coriolanus did not figure anywhere in the annual list of magistrates. And it was a legend which was inordinately embellished by the Marcian family during its rise in the late fourth century. Even the name Coriolanus is perplexing, because it would have been wildly anachronistic at that date for him to have acquired it as a result of his heroism at the capture of Corioli (as Livy and others maintain), whereas if he were a citizen of Corioli his presence and position at Rome is equally inexplicable. More-

over the whole legend has been overlaid with Greek parallels. Coriolanus is a second Themistocles who turns against his country (Cicero, *Brutus* 41). The meeting between Coriolanus and his mother is elaborated to evoke the celebrated encounter between Jocasta and her sons in the Oedipus legend.

All I think that can be maintained is that the legend does reflect Volscian activity against Rome in the first quarter of the century and that that activity posed a very real threat to the actual existence of Rome. Coriolanus made two attacks on Rome, the first from Circeii along the Via Latina, capturing Tolerium, Bola, Labici, Pedum, Corbio and Bovillae and reaching the outskirts of Rome, the second through coastal Latium, capturing Longula, Satricum, Setia, Pollusca, Corioli and Mugilla (so Dionysius 8.14-36; Livy 2.39). How the names of the individual towns were remembered (perhaps in song or oral memory?) and whether, indeed, they have been historically remembered cannot now be proved. But the strength of the legend is the reality of the threat which the Volscians made to Rome.

3. The final indication is a mutilated notice in Festus (180L.), who records the names of nine people who were killed in battle against the Volscians and cremated, probably in 487 BC. He seems to have been recording an inscription but, since the nine people are listed with their *cognomina* (which was a fourth-century phenomenon : cf. Coriolanus above), the copy which he (or rather his source, presumably Verrius Flaccus) consulted must have been a more recent restoration. Nevertheless it affords independent and authentic evidence for the magnitude of the danger.

> [Nine tribunes of the soldiers in the army of]
> T. Sicinius (cos. 437 BC) when the Volsci
> [rebelled and] organized [a fierce battle] against
> [the Romans] [were killed and] are said to have
> been cremated [in the Cir]cus [and were buried
> there in an enclosu]re near the Circ[us]
> [which was afterwards] paved with white stone.
> [Those who died for the State were] Opiter Verginius
> [Tricostus (cos. 502)] [M. or M'. Valerius] Laevinus,
> Postumius Co[minius Auruncus (cos. 493)]

[M'. Tu]llius Tolerinus (cos. 500), P. Ve[turius
(cos. 499)], [A. Sempr]onius Atratinus (cos. 491),
Ver[ginius Tircostus (cos. 494 or 496)]
[P. Mu]tius Scaevola, Sex. Fusi[us (cos. 488)]

Some confirmation of the threat to the physical existence of Rome itself is given by the construction of the first defensive wall. Traditionally this was ascribed to Servius Tullius (Livy 1.44.3), but in fact the surviving Republican wall is of fourth-century date, built, presumably, after the Gallic sack. There was however an earlier earth-rampart (*agger*) which has been dated by a small Red-Figure sherd to *c*. 490-470 BC. This seems to have been the original defence of the city, though whether it found a complete circle is uncertain. In the times of the Tarquins Rome did not need protection: in the troubled times after 500 BC Rome, in common with other cities, had to look to her own preservation. Significantly the first walls at Veii also belong to a period a little before 450 BC (see p. 148).

But much the most serious threat came from the Latins themselves. Assailed as Rome was by the Sabines and the Volscians (and, no doubt, others such as the Aequi and Hernici as well) she found herself in a desperate position as the result of the determined stand taken by her former 'allies' or dependants no longer to accept her leadership. A new league of Latin cities, separate and distinct from Rome, was established, and the bitter feud between Rome and this alliance had to be settled before the Latins could once again mount a common defence against their enemies. The dispute was resolved by a decisive battle in 496 BC at Lake Regillus, where the Roman hoplite infantry proved superior to the predominantly cavalry tactics of the Latins.

There is some external evidence for the Latin alliance, apart from the literary narrative preserved by Livy, Dionysius and others. At Pratica di Mare, the site of the ancient Lavinium, there have been found since the war the remains of a huge sanctuary, containing at least thirteen archaic altars of local tufa. (There were probably more but the precise number is as yet undetermined.) Some of the altars have been rebuilt, but the earliest of them can be dated to about 500 BC (or marginally earlier); and that is probably the date of the sanctuary as a whole. The altars are constructed and aligned on fundamentally Greek (as opposed to Etruscan or Italic) principles. Apart from one early inscription, considered below, (and one third-century inscription, which falls outside our period), there is no indication of the deities worshipped at these altars, but it has been argued, on the basis of analogy, that it was a major federal sanctuary, the religious centre of a league.

At some point in history Lavinium, in deliberate competition with Rome, claimed Aeneas for herself. The claim was already established by the time of the poet Lycophron (*Alex.* 1250-60; c. 290 BC) who refers to the miracle of the sow and thirty piglets which appeared to Aeneas at Lavinium, and it became part of the agreed tradition of Roman pre-history, adopted by Varro and Vergil (*Aeneid* 1.2-3; *et al.*). A few years ago an inscription was found at Tor Tignosa, some five miles from Lavinium, near the River Numicus (where Aeneas is said to have disappeared from mortal sight), which reads *Lare Aineia D[ono* or *onum]*. It dates from about 300 BC and confirms a literary tradition that Aeneas was worshipped in the locality as Aeneas Indiges. Dr Weinstock was right to argue that both Lar and Indiges are to be interpreted as 'deified ancestor'. I suspect that when Lavinium set itself up in opposition to Rome it tried to arrogate the Aeneas myth and to invest itself with all the grandeur of Trojan association.

The archaic dedication from the 'federal sanctuary' is more clear-cut : Castorei Podlouqueique qurois – 'to Castor and Pollux, the young men (qurois = Gk. Kourois)'. Now there are two significant features about the cult of Castor and Pollux. They were pre-eminently the patrons of horses. They are also worshipped at this time in other Latin communities which are known to have opposed Rome at the Battle of Lake Regillus. Tusculum was a centre of their cult (Cicero, *On Divination* 1.98; Festus 408L.). Ardea had an archaic shrine to them (Servius, on *Aeneid* 1.44), and they were honoured at Praeneste (Servius, on *Aeneid* 7.678) and Cora (*CIL* 1.2.1506).

With this archaeological background it is possible to turn to what the Romans wrote about Lake Regillus itself.

No even remotely specious reason is given for the outbreak of hostilities, beyond the statement (Livy 2.18.2) that
'it was generally agreed that Octavius Mamilius was stirring
up the thirty Latin peoples', presumably to engineer the
restoration of his father-in-law, Tarquin. The battle itself
is described by Livy and Dionysius in purely Homeric terms,
as Lord Macaulay perceived. The details are modelled on the
doings of Paris and Menelaus, Agamemnon and Hector, and
Nestor in the *Iliad*. All this means is that there was no
genuine account of the battle at all. Why should there have
been? But certain things were remembered, perhaps through
the family of the Postumii who certainly continued for
many centuries to claim hereditary credit for the victory.

The first was that it was fought at Lake Regillus, which is
close to Tusculum – probably Pontano Secco, two miles north
of Frascati. The site is relevant because it implies that the
Romans were taking the offensive and were aiming to strike
at Tusculum, one of the leading cities of the Latin league
(see p. 77).

The second was that it involved a substantial number of the
Latin communities. Livy gives the nominal figure of thirty
but the truth is more probably that the figure thirty was
at all times a theoretical number in the fortunes of the
Latin league and that only a quorum of involved states in
fact sided with Tusculum and Lavinium in the battle. Nevertheless, the split is clear enough.

Thirdly the dictator A. Postumius Albus vowed a temple to
the Dioscuri, Castor and Pollux, in the heat of the battle and
that temple was in fact dedicated in 484 BC. The Romans won
the battle; and in establishing the cult of Castor and Pollux
they no doubt hoped to deprive the Latins of the support of
their military deities, and also to convince the reactionary
patrons of cavalry-warfare of the superior advantage of
infantry tactics. It corresponded to what the Romans called
an *exoratio*, by which a deity's allegiance could be alienated
and transferred to the Roman side (see p. 156).

It must have been a battle against great odds, fought with
all the daring of desperation, but its results were incalculable.
The immediate and major conseq*t*ence was that the Latins
agreed to sign a treaty with Ro*t*ne which provided for a

common defensive alliance on a basis of equality. A copy of the treaty is known to have stood in the Forum, inscribed on a bronze column, until the first century BC. It is referred to by both Cicero (*pro Balbo* 53) and Livy (2.33.9.). But it cannot be proved whether it was the original document, or a modernized and revised version of it. It certainly contained the name of Sp. Cassius and this was used to fix the date to 493 BC, his first consulship, but he may have figured in the text as *fetial* rather than consul (see p. 83) and hence the treaty may belong closer in date to the actual battle – i.e. 496-5 BC.

The terms of the treaty are quoted by Dionysius (6.95.2).

1. There shall be peace between Rome and all the Latin cities, so long as heaven and earth shall maintain their same position. They shall neither themselves make war against each other nor introduce wars from elsewhere, nor allow right of access to aggressors.
2. They shall bring all available help to those who are attacked.
3. Each party shall have an equal share of the spoils and booty from common wars.
4. Judgement in private commercial cases shall be given within ten days, in the place in which the contract was made.
5. Nothing shall be added or removed from the terms of the treaty except with the approval of Rome and all the Latins.

(Two small Latin quotations in Festus 166L. probably were part of the financial and legal stipulations in 4.)

There has been much dispute whether the terms as set out by Dionysius can have been original. The general provisions about peace and neutrality are relatively standard but there are some oddities.

1. The duration ('so long as heaven and earth abide') is almost unparalleled. The nearest equivalent is in a treaty made by Alexander the Great with the Celts in 335 BC. The normal phrase would be 'for ever'.

2. The division of the spoils has been regarded as un-authentic, but it has received recent confirmation from the fragmentary text of the treaty between Rome and Aetolia concluded in 212 BC (SEG 13.382) which specifies that the movable booty from captured cities should be shared between the two allies, not to go solely to the Romans (as was usual). Since Rome was not negotiating with the Latins from a position of overwhelming supremacy and since the alliance provided for joint commands and joint forces the provision for dividing the spoils seems reasonable.

3. The trading clause is unusual. On the one hand such private law provisos do not normally figure in public treaties and secondly the commercial relationships would normally be covered by the public institution of *commercium*, that is to say a treaty obligation which establishes the right of a Tusculan, for example, to make contracts with a Roman enforceable in Roman courts according to Roman law and vice versa. Nevertheless, when seen against the particular economic difficulties of the 490s which are discussed below, this provision cannot be dismissed out of hand.

On balance, therefore, most scholars accept the text of the treaty as given by Dionysius as being substantially genuine (if perhaps modernized and not wholly complete).

There are two remaining questions. How numerous were the Latin communities with which Rome made the treaty? And how effectively was the defensive alliance organized?

Dionysius (5.61) says that thirty towns were involved and this, at some stage, became the traditional number, as recorded by Livy and, for example, in the prodigy of the thirty piglets. He indeed gives a list of names but there is a suspicion that some of the names (e.g. Setia, Circeii, Norba) are anachronistic. His list is: Ardea, Aricia, Boillae (presumably Bovillae), Bubentum, Corni (?Corani=Cora), Carventum, Lavinium, Lanuvium, Circeii, Corioli, Corbio, Cabum, Fortinii, Gabii, Laurentum, Labici, Nomentum, Norba, Praeneste, Pedum, Querquetulum, Satricum, Scaptia, Setia, Tibur, Tusculum, Tolerium, Tellenae and Velitrae. The list only in fact contains twenty-nine names. One may have been lost in transmission, perhaps Pometia or even Tarracina. Or he may have

THE TEN AFFILIATE MEMBERS OF THE LATIN LEAGUE

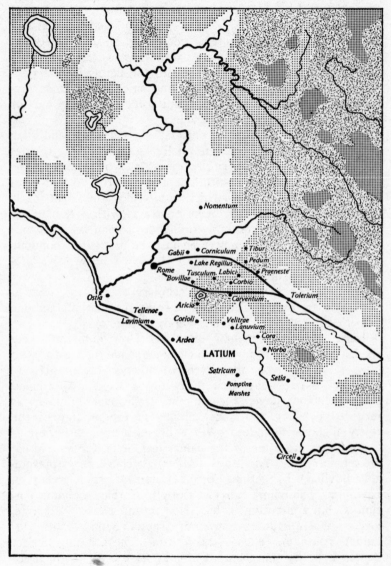

Nomentum

Gabii • Corniculum • Tibur
• Lake Regillus • Pedum
Rome • Tusculum. Labici: • Praeneste
Bovillae • Corbio

Ostia Carventum Tolerium

Tellenae Aricia
Lavinium Corioli Velitrae
• Lanuvium
• Ardea • Cora
• Norba

LATIUM

Satricum Setia
Pomptine
Marshes

Circeii

included Rome herself among the thirty. Moreover, it is virtually certain that no such place as Laurentum existed any longer, and that the Laurentes formed a joint community with Lavinium, like the Rutuli at Ardea. Many of the places figure in the Volscian campaigns of Coriolanus, and there is some separate but ambiguous information about Praeneste which is reported to have defected to the Romans in 499 BC (Livy 2.19.2); although I suspect that this is no more than a quite independent survival of the fact that Praeneste joined the Latin alliance with Rome.

Other lists of Latin communities exist, including a much later one given by Livy of thirty Roman colonies in 209 BC (27.9.7), but since none of these lists even purport to have anything to do with Lake Regillus and Cassius' treaty, it is safer to ignore them entirely. The probability is that most of the peoples listed by Dionysius signed the treaty at once or in the following decade. Fundamentally it amounted to a reorganization of the old Roman-Latin league engineered by the Tarquins, with Rome's dominating role severely cut down in size. The treaty remained in force down to 338 BC by which time there were still thirteen effective signatories.

The practical effect of the treaty was to provide for a federal army for the defence of Latium. One valuable piece of evidence about it is preserved by the antiquarian Cincius (in Festus 276L.) who is discussing the habit by which a praetor, setting out to govern a province in the capacity of pro-praetor or pro-consul, is greeted at the gate.

Until the consulship of P. Decius Mus (240 BC), the Latin peoples used to meet at the Fountain of Ferentina (near Aricia: continuity with the old league of Diana is implied) and to decide jointly on matters involving the supreme command. So in the year that it was the responsibility of the Romans to send commanders to the army on the instructions of the Latins, a number of Roman citizens used to watch from day-break on the Capitol for the signs given by birds. When the birds gave their verdict, the soldier who had been sent for the purpose by the Latin league used to greet as commander (praetor) the man whom the birds had singled out as the person to take charge of the area of responsibility with supreme command.

This ceremony must be derived from the early workings of
the Latin league. It presupposes that there was a rotation
system for selecting the commanders of the Latin army (there
were normally two praetors: Livy 8.3.9) and that Rome took
its turn in that rota. We hear, for instance, of T. Quinctius
being sent out as 'pro-consul' (i.e. Latin praetor) with an
allied army in 464 BC to face the Aequi (Livy 3.4.10). It presupposes also that a regular army was on stand-by each year,
with contingents available both from Rome and from the
Latin allies. It would be used as and when circumstances
dictated. Gradually, of course, Rome came to acquire over-
riding authority in the League and the old equality became
a mere memory of the past; but for at least fifty years the
alliance set up by Sp. Cassius helped to ensure the safety
and prosperity of Latium in the face of taxing threats.

Although by 490 BC the military situation in Latium had
been stabilized, this did little to mitigate the desperate
domestic problems at Rome.

The collapse of the Tarquin dynasty had repercussions not
only on the international scene but also on Rome's domestic
economy. Long-established trade-routes, such as that to Campania, were broken and trade suffered general disruption.
Even the valuable salt-business, on which much of Rome's
prosperity depended, is likely to have been interrupted by
the incursions of Porsenna and the series of Sabine wars
which menaced the route by which the salt was conveyed
(the Via Salaria). An obscure notice in Livy for the third
year of the Republic (2.9.6) speaks of public control being
imposed on the price of salt. This may reflect something
of the difficulties which Rome was facing.

Another indication of the same critical situation can be
derived from studying the import of pottery into Rome over
a number of years. There is, inevitably, an element of random
chance in the distribution of finds which are made; but the
trend is too well marked as a whole to be accidental. Fragments of over 200 imported Greek vases have been discovered
in Rome belonging to the period 530-500 BC. The great majority

of them are Attic (171 Black Figure, 20 Red Figure), but there is also some Ionian ware and one fragment which may be Laconian. For the next fifty years (500-450 BC), a period almost twice as long, only 145 imported vases have been found, all Attic. A similar decline can be detected in the local pottery. In Gjerstad's words, 'the time of inspired work- manship has passed : the Bucchero pottery . . . assume[s] more and more a debased character. Ordinary Bucchero is gradually transported into the hopelessly ever-grey Subarchaic Bucchero and a ceramic new-comer with painted ornaments is the Coarse Painted ware. The very name tells what it is.'

The decline was partly peculiar to Rome, but it is also reflected over most of Latium and Etruria, as the excavations at San Giovenale show. Society and trade in central Italy as a whole were badly dislocated, and the Etruscan stake in Cam- pania became increasingly precarious until it was virtually eliminated in 474 BC by the Syracusan victory at the Battle of Cumae. As far as Rome itself was concerned, the distress was aggravated by a series of bad harvests which forced the Romans to buy corn abroad, in Etruria, Cumae or even Sicily. Crop failure and the price of corn (*annona*) were items regularly mentioned in the Annales (Cato fr. 77P.) so that there is no reason to doubt the authenticity of the notices about it from the early Republic, even if there may be some latitude in the actual dates recorded; the countries from which relief was sought reflect the Etruscan character of Rome and her ties with Carthage, which had a substantial footing in Sicily. Such notices are recorded for the third year of the Republic and then under 499, 492, 486, 477 and 476 BC (in traditional dates). The Annales also preserved notices about disease, from which it can be inferred that during the century there were a number of severe epidemics. The earliest recorded was 490 BC. Bad years in 463 and 453 were the prelude to a disastrous decade between 437 and 428 BC which severely inhibited Rome's progress (see p. 138). It is not possible at this distance to diagnose these diseases, but the fact that some of them were said to have attacked animals as well as men points to anthrax as a strong possibility. One other phenomenon must not be overlooked. It is certain that malaria became endemic in the northern Mediterranean during the

fifth century; it was no doubt encouraged by the draining of
the salt-lakes at Ostia and by the extent of the Pomptine
marshes. It is worth noting that the Volscians are said to
have been attacked by disease when operating near the
Pomptine marshes in 490 BC (Livy 2.34.5), and their resulting
weakness no doubt contributed as much to their eventual
failure as the concerted defence put up by the Latins and
Romans. Malaria also accounted for the disappearance of
some of the low-lying Latin communities, such as Longula and
Pollusca, during the fifth century.

Bad harvests and disease figure in the pontifical chronicles.
But even without that evidence, we could have guessed the
truth from the spate of temple-dedications during these years.
At first sight it is unexpected that Rome could afford to
erect lavish temples if she was economically strained. And it
is no explanation to point out that this was a generation all
over the Etruscanized world, for which temple-building was
fashionable. Velletri, Pyrgi, Satricum and Veii are other cities
which witnessed the construction of imposing temples at
this time. Whatever the fashion may have been, the motive
stemmed from need and anxiety, and the nature of those
needs can be ascertained by considering which deities were
honoured.

1. In 497 BC a temple was built to Saturn (Livy 2.21.2),
probably on the site of an earlier altar (Festus 430L.). The
original function of Saturn was obscured by his later identification with the Greek Kronos, and by the misguided attempt
of Roman scholars to associate his name with *sata* – crops.
The name Saturn is Etruscan and its meaning unknown, but
his primitive sphere of operation can be discovered from the
fact that in archaic prayers, the special power, which was
invoked, was the Lua Saturni (Livy 8.1.6; Varro, *On the Latin
Language* 8.36; Aul. Gell. 13.23). Lua must be connected with
luo, lues, lustrum etc. and denote the power to free, cleanse,
purify from disease. It was no doubt against blight that
Saturn was invoked.

2. A temple of Mercury was dedicated in 495 BC (Livy
2.21.6, 27.5). There was a myth that the people took the law
into their own hands and entrusted the dedication of the
temple not to the consuls but to a plebeian soldier, M.

Laetorius. No weight should be put on this, except perhaps that it may commemorate the concern shown by the plebeians in the cult. For there is no doubt that it was designed to stimulate trade.

3. The temple of Ceres, however, vowed in 496 BC and dedicated in 493 BC was predominantly plebeian. Neither the date nor the nature of the cult can seriously be disputed, although Professor Alföldi has attempted to deny the traditional chronology. Known by the single name of Ceres, the temple in fact held a triad of deities – Ceres, Liber and Libera, who were derived from the Greek deities, Demeter, Dionysus and Persephone. The inspiration for the cult came undoubtedly from Cumae where Demeter was a leading goddess and her priesthood much prized. The Greek bias is further accentuated by the fact that the temple was designed in a Greek style and the names of two Greek artists who were responsible for its ornamentation, Damophon and Gorgasos, were inscribed on it (Pliny, *Natural History* 35.154). The plebeian associations are numerous. It was at the foot of the Aventine, a traditionally plebeian hill (Livy 3.31.1); it was superintended by the plebeian aediles (3.55.13: the name aedile probably originally denoted the custodian of a temple); the fines imposed by plebeian tribunes were used for its upkeep (10.23.13); and the tribunes themselves were protected by the authority of Ceres, and anyone who violated them was judged forfeit to Ceres (Dionysius 6.89: Livy 3.55.13 prefers Jupiter).

Two important conclusions follow. The cult must have been instituted as a reaction to the corn-shortages which have already been noticed. Secondly, the chief sufferers seem to have been the plebeians and in setting up a cult largely of their own and in looking to Greece for their inspiration, both religious and political, they reveal the violence and the inner tensions at Rome during this period.

Those tensions finally erupted in civil disobedience. Hunger and poverty, resulting from the depressed conditions since 505 BC and the unsettled world around, had already exasperated the poorer classes. And in such times the poor get poorer and the rich richer. This may explain why Cassius' treaty contained exceptional provisions for the rapid settling of commercial disputes. But the position was made worse at Rome by the existence of a severe debt-procedure – *nexum* – which survived down to the fourth century. The exact system is nowhere fully described but it can be reconstructed chiefly from a long note by Varro (*On the Latin Language* 7.105) which ends: 'a free man who gives his services into slavery in exchange for the money which he owes (which is weighed out before five witnesses on a scale – *per aes et libram*), is called *nexus* until he has repaid it.' The debtor transferred his services to his creditor in settlement of the debt. He did indeed technically retain his civic rights, for in Roman law you could only sell your services, not yourself, but effectively you became a bondsman (*nexus*), and could be exploited or maltreated at will. And this bondage was in no sense conditional or temporary: it was once for all, unless a third party came and bought your services back off your creditor and so released you. For in a world without money, there were few ways of discharging a debt once it had been incurred. The number of *nexi* and their plight was one of the most lamentable features of early Roman society.

If it had just been an explosion between rich and poor, the events of 494 BC – the so-called First Secession of the Plebs – would be easy to understand. What happened can be recovered with some degree of probability, although the story evolved and grew as successive historians handled it, and wrote contemporary political overtones into it. Early versions are given by Cicero (*On the Republic* 2.58: perhaps from Polybius) and by L. Calpurnius Piso (consul in 133 BC). The later versions, which survive in full in Livy and Dionysius, have been embroidered by the political and artistic sympathies of the Sullan writers, Licinius Macer and Valerius Antias.

A body of plebeians withdrew to the Aventine and 'struck'. By an old Italic custom they swore a communal oath of mutual self-help: a very similar oath is later recorded of the Samnites. After negotiations with the Senate and the consuls, the plebeians agreed to return on condition that two officers, tribunes of the plebs or *tribuni plebis*, should be elected by the *comitia curiata*, whose role was basically to protect individuals from arrest or molestation (*auxilium*). That power derived not from legal sanction so much as from the assurance that the people would rally to their support, and that anyone who violated them could be judged forfeit to Ceres (i.e. could be lynched with impunity). The first two tribunes were L. Sicinius and L. Albinius – both Etruscan names.

Two features about the story, which was so much a part of popular political mythology that its outline is unlikely to be false, are particularly striking: the name and number of the tribunes, and their election by the *curiae*. The name must have been modelled on the military tribunes, who commanded the units of 1,000 men (*chiliarcho*i in Greek). Varro indeed sees this, although his explanation is rather different (*On the Latin Language* 5.81 : 'tribunes of the plebs because they were first created from the tribunes of the soldiers, to defend the plebs'). And their number, two, balances the two consuls. Their election by the *curiae*, rather than by the *comitia centuriata*, again suggests distrust of the established military organization. Until their own tribal assembly was created in 471 BC, the poorer plebeians would be reluctant to entrust the election of their own officers to a body whose membership was based on wealth, and who alone were able to profit from the troubled war-time conditions of the present, as the provision in Cassius' treaty about the distribution of spoils makes all too clear.

The quarrel, therefore, at first appears to have been one between the rich (the *classis*) and the poor (the *infra classem*) and might be thought to support Momigliano's view of the true significance of the term 'plebeian' (discussed above p. 58).

Alternatively, one might be tempted to distinguish a conscious movement against an Etruscan or Etruscanized aristocracy. The poor looked to the Greek world – that home of democratic ideas or, their close equivalent, popular tyranny. Did the connection with Cumae appeal to the plebs at least partly because Tarquin, the people's friend, was residing there in exile? Certainly there are Etruscan names in the early Fasti, and certainly the years up to 490 BC are marked by good relations with the major cities of south Etruria. And the hoplite army was essentially an Etruscan invention. Yet there is no evidence for a dramatic break with Etruria after 490 BC and there is nothing in the sources which indicates that the quarrel was in any way ethnic. Why were Albinius and Sicinius elected tribunes?

Historical tradition always regarded the quarrel as being between the two religio-social classes, the patricians and the plebeians, but the patricians by themselves, that is the descendants of members of the regal Senate, would obviously have been numerically much inferior. By virtue of inherited religious rights (especially the *auspicia*, the secret control of the law and the calendar, the administration of the major cults, and, perhaps, the monopoly of the consulship), they might, as a united class, run an exclusive and authoritarian government, but only with the help of a substantial body of dependants. And this is precisely what the great patrician families had. As the Claudii and later the Fabii attest, a patrician could count on a large retinue of clients, who owed service to him in exchange for the protection which they received, such as support at law, which would serve them in good stead if the danger of *nexum* were to arise. Festus (228L.) also indicates that the patricians bought the allegiance of poorer people by allotting them small holdings of land to cultivate. It was the small independent trader, craftsman, artist, smallholder who fared worst in times of crisis and who had no powerful patron to turn to for assistance. Such people might well be Etruscan, as most of the craftsman were, but they need not have been. What they were was poor and vulnerable – and plebeian. They did not have access to the religious keys of government.

The settlement with the Latins, the repulse of the Volscians and the concessions which successfully ended the first Secession restored a measure of stability to Rome which it had not enjoyed for twenty years. It is true that the Volscians remained a threat. It is also true that a few years later, in 486 BC, Sp. Cassius, perhaps exploiting his popularity in having negotiated the treaty with the Latins, is said to have tried to take advantage of the corn-shortage to set himself up as tyrant. But the attempt was abortive and historically is of no significance. The settled conditions enabled Rome to stem the economic decline and to hold her own as an autonomous and respected community on the Tiber. Significantly the temple of Castor and Pollux was dedicated in 484 BC.

The campaigns associated with the name of Coriolanus re-present the high-water mark of the Volscian invasion. The Vol-scians still occupied Roman attention after 485 BC and could pose a threat from time to time, but their thrust had lost its impetus. The Pomptine marshes hampered their movement and, perhaps, debilitated their forces. By 470 BC the Romans had recovered the initiative and were operating against Antium itself (Livy 2.63-65). The more serious dangers now lay further north. The Romans made an effective alliance in 486 BC with the Hernici, who formed a wedge between the Volscians and the Aequi, an Oscan hill-people like the Volscians who threatened the upper reaches of the River Tolerus, which carried the Via Latina and the main route from Etruria past Praeneste to the south. The Aequi have left little trace archaeologically, but their record is one of persistent incur-sion into Latium and of bitter skirmishing for the control of the eastern edge of the Alban hills, especially the pass of Algidus. They are first heard of as serious enemies in 488 BC. (Livy 2.40.12) and they maintain an unremitting struggle for over fifty years, sometimes by themselves, sometimes in league with the Volscians or the Sabines. The individual details of the struggle are unimportant. It was mainly the frontier-towns of Latium, such as Tusculum and Corbio, which bore the brunt of the fighting. The one famous emergency, which summoned Cincinnatus from the plough (Livy 3.26) is a time-less legend, whose circumstances have been entirely fabri-cated to give him a crisis worthy of his mettle.

The Sabines on the other hand were a greater source of anxiety, not just because they commanded the Via Salaria and could menace Rome itself more directly. This they did in fact do on several occasions. In 496 BC a party of marauders reached the gates of Rome (Livy 2.63.7); and in the follow-ing years they burned and plundered the *ager* Crustuminus and the country around the river Anio before advancing once more to the gates (Livy 2.64.3). In 460 BC a group of Sabines

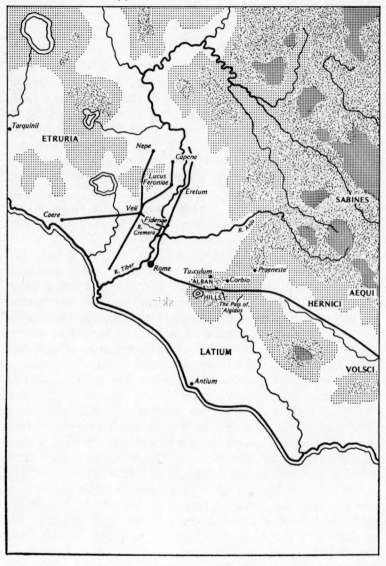

LATIUM *Circa* 470 B.C.

and others (the Roman historians denigrated them as slaves and exiles) under Appius Herdonius, succeeded in seizing the Capitol at Rome and were only eventually dislodged with the help of a Latin allied contingent from Tusculum (Livy 3.15.18). Two years later they were able once again to mount a big attack on Rome.

Part of the secret of the Sabine success was that they had an effective understanding with the Veientes on the other side of the Tiber. One of the important Sabine strong-holds, Eretum, which lies astride the Via Salaria, guards a major crossing of the river. A road leads towards it from the Etruscan centres of Capena and Lucus Feroniae, and the influence of Etruscan culture is very evident in the fifth-century pottery fragments from Eretum. It is therefore no surprise to find a Sabine contingent camped at Veii in 475 BC or to read that a joint Etruscan-Sabine force was planning to cooperate with Appius Herdonius.

It was no doubt as an attempt to distract this pressure by diplomatic means that the consul Sp. Postumius associated the Sabine god Sancus with the old cult of Dius Fidius in 466 BC. Dionysius (9.60.8) reports the event slightly differently in that he says that the shrine which had been founded by Tarquin had not been properly dedicated until Sp. Postumius solemnized it, but the evidence is clear that the original cult was simply that of Dius Fidius and that the identification with Sancus was added later, well before the third century. That Sancus was a Sabine god, who watched over oaths and good faith, is stated by several authors whose special knowledge must command belief (Dionysius 2.49.2, quoting the elder Cato; Varro, *On the Latin Language* 5.66, quoting the early second-century scholar Aelius Stilo). (The final addition to the god's title of Semo – Semo Sancus Dius Fidius – belongs to the fourth century: Livy 8.20.8.) The attempt thus to consolidate Sabine support was clearly abortive.

For the Veientes were a new, and potentially very dangerous, adversary. The Sabines, Volscians and Aequi were predominantly nomadic: their tactics were the primitive tactics of cattle-raiders. But Veii was a civilized Etruscan city – a match for Rome. It was built on a rocky plateau, nearly two miles long and three-quarters of a mile wide at its widest. At the southern end was the citadel (Piazza d'Armi), at the foot of which the river Cremera (Valchetta), which flows around the eastern side of the city, is joined by the Fosso dei due Fosse which runs round the western side. The city was thus surrounded by water and by towering cliffs, apart from a small neck of land to the north-west. Its site is huge and appears almost impregnable. Veii lay about twelve miles from Rome and its territory reached the Tiber. It was the centre of an elaborate road-system : roads radiated out to the saltbeds at the Tiber mouth, to Caere, Nepe, Tarquinii, Vulci, Capena and Rome.

Veii's geographical position contributed to its early prosperity. From the middle of the sixth century it was a flourishing artistic centre, specializing in terracottas. It was from Veii that the artists were invited to decorate the Capitoline temple at Rome, and impressive remains have been discovered at Veii itself. Two shrines have been found in the citadel; and a spectacular temple, with statues of Apollo, Hercules and other deities, has been excavated at the Portonaccio site just outside the western walls. The streets of the city were laid out on a grid-system and the houses were evidently built with stone foundations and brick walls.

During the sixth century and the early years of the fifth, relations between Rome and Veii seem to have been friendly. The first mention of hostilities comes in 483 BC when the Veientes began a series of annual raids on Roman territory. How is the change to be explained? Probably the single main factor was the decline of Etruscan influence in Campania, which had afforded Etruscan merchants their principal outlet to Greek markets. There is a marked drop in the quantity and quality of Veientane products from about 480 BC which is matched by the reduced scale of imports from Greece. In addition the inroads of the Volscians will have affected communications to the south and cut them off even more from Magna Graecia. Veii, in short, was feeling the pinch, and the recovery which Rome started to make aggravated the position, particularly if the salt-trade was once more flowing along the Via Salaria; for Rome and Veii, with saltbeds south and north of the Tiber mouth respectively, were rival suppliers to the great inland cities. Veii's aim was to curtail that trade and to hinder the expansion of Rome. To achieve that her foothold across the Tiber at Fidenae and her alliance with the Sabines were strategically essential.

There is no evidence of any anti-Roman or anti-Etruscan animosity as such yet, but it cannot be a coincidence that between 485 BC and 479 BC a member of the Fabian family was always consul. For the Fabii had particular ties with Etruria. As late as 310 BC there is a record of a Fabius, brother or half-brother of the consul Q. Fabius Rullianus, being educated at Caere and speaking fluent Etruscan (Livy 9.36.3). The Fabii in the fourth century were in fact responsible for penetrating and winning over Etruria; and this historical tradition is confirmed by local discoveries, such as a bilingual text from Clusium inscribed Au. Fapi. Larthial – A. Fabi. Iucnes. And even earlier when the Gauls had reached as far as Clusium on their southward push in 391 BC the inhabitants asked Rome for help; the Romans answered by sending an embassy of three Fabii to investigate the situation and to remonstrate with the Gauls (Livy 5.35.36).

The evidence is not easy to evaluate. It could be argued that the presence of the Fabii so regularly in the Fasti indicates an aggressive policy adopted by a group at Rome, who aimed to extend Roman influence into south Etruria now that the situation in Latium had been stabilized. But I suspect that such an interpretation is too elaborate. Rome was far from strong or secure; and the forays of the Sabines suggest that it is more likely that the Veientes were also seeking to exploit her difficulties. If so, the Fabii will have been endeavouring, through their Etruscan connections, to maintain good relations with south Etruria and to contain the Veientes. It is even possible that some of the Fabian land adjoined the *ager* Veientanus, which would have given the Fabii a particular responsibility for peace-keeping. At all events, once hostilities had commenced in 483 BC, the conflict was fierce. The sources record skirmishes and raids in 482 and 481 BC, culminating in a major battle in 480 BC in which Q. Fabius was killed and two other Fabii, including the consul M. Fabius, eventually saved the day. The details of the battle are demonstrably fictitious. It provides the background for the decision

to man a small frontier post on the river Cremera to control
the road leading from Veii down to the Tiber. That story has
become so overlaid with Herodotean parallels borrowed from
the Battle of Thermopylae that it is quite impossible to reconstruct what actually happened. The 306 Fabii and their dependants are the Spartans and their allies dressed up in Roman
clothes. All that can be said is that a Fabian attempt to
bottle up Veii was decisively defeated and for several years
following Veientine detachments ravaged the outskirts of
Rome with impunity. In association with the Sabines they
posed a threat of the utmost gravity. But, surprisingly, in
474 BC they concluded a truce with Rome (Livy 2.54.1). The
sources say that the truce was for forty years but the duration is likely to be imaginary, being inferred from the next
recorded outbreak of war (437 BC: Livy 4.17.8). The truce itself,
however, is genuine and was largely motivated by the shock
of crushing defeat suffered by the Etruscans at the Battle
of Cumae.

Whatever the precise circumstances, the war with Veii was
a turning-point in Rome's history. Veii was to dominate her
horizon for the next 100 years, and, until finally captured in
396 BC, prevented Rome from developing her trade and
contact with south Etruria. It is, therefore, probably not
fanciful to believe that during those years a consciousness
of specifically Roman identity – an identity distinct from
Etruscan or Latin – grew up. Etruscan inscriptions are no
longer found at Rome; Etruscan imports diminish still further
and more or less cease after 450 BC. Perhaps still more significantly a number of Etruscan names disappear for good.
What happened to the Larcii, the Cominii, the Cassii, to name
but three families that provided prominent figures in the
early Republic and then are not heard of again after about
480 BC? Some of them may have died out; but some may
have emigrated back to Etruria.

Such was the external background against which Rome's
political evolution should be seen. Once the immediate danger
posed by Veii had passed in 474 BC Rome had still the harass-
ment of the Sabines and the Aequi to face; but the Latins and
the Hernici appear to have remained loyal, and the Volscians

were past their peak. It was not a peaceful period, but equally it was no longer a time of crisis; and it allowed a new generation to reflect how little the Secession of the plebs and the creation of the tribunes had in reality achieved. Unfortunately there are no documented facts to illustrate what the specific grievances were. In a sense the problems will have remained the same – debts, corn-shortages, poor business, obscure laws, and the unfair advantage enjoyed by the patricians (and their dependants) over the plebeians. And, at first, the only remedy for the plebeians seemed to be to improve on the concessions which they had already won. In 471 BC they succeeded in establishing a third assembly based upon the tribes (as opposed to centuries or curias) as voting units for which only plebeians were eligible. The purpose of this, as both Livy (3.58.1) and Dionysius (9.41) make clear, was to prevent patricians from being able to influence the voting so as to appoint amenable or corruptible tribunes. Secondly, the number of tribunes was increased from two to either four (Diodorus 11.68.8) or five (Piso: Livy 2.58.1). Four is more probable since the fifth name, L. Maecilius, looks like a mere duplication of the fourth, Icilius, and the number four probably reflects the four urban tribes which would have contained the greatest majority of plebeians requiring protection and assistance. The two events belong together and the traditional date is reasonable. It must have been before 450 BC because the Twelve Tables, in speaking of the greatest assembly (*maximus comitiatus*), imply the existence of three assemblies, and it is likely to have been after the truce with Veii had brought a breathing-space. The names C. Sicinius (or Cn. Siccius), L. Numitorius, M. Duilius and Sp. Icilius are adequately authentic.

Two factors, however, must have helped to alter the general position. Rome's emergence as an independent power brought her increasingly into contact with the Greek world, notably Cumae and the Sicilian cities from which she bought corn. Greek influence has already been seen in the circumstances attending the institution of the cult of Ceres. Moreover, the Persian Wars had brought Magna Graecia and mainland Greece, above all Athens, closer together. Athenian ideas of democracy were beginning to spread over the Mediterranean. Not the least important consequence of the actions of Pericles and Ephialtes in 463 BC was the sudden flurry of publication of laws and decrees. Democracy had to be seen as well as heard in action, if it was to be true democracy. These Greek ideas were not lost on the leaders of the Roman people. Secondly, by 460 BC, it had become clear that the patriciate was a fixed, closed body. Since there were no longer kings, there could no longer be newly ennobled patricians: for it was part of the prerogative of a sacral monarchy to create patricians. Any thrusting and successful plebeian, who might have had a chance of recognition as the head of a family deserving a place in the Senate and so becoming patrician under the kings, was now permanently debarred. It will have taken a generation to see these consequences of the expulsion of the Tarquins.

Mere self-help, the rough-and-ready defensive mechanisms of the tribunate, were not going to do more than protect individuals from outstanding injustice and abuse. The patricians held the keys of government because they alone had the religious control of the law and all that went with it (the calendar, the auspices etc.). For the plebeians to make any advance they had to have open access to knowledge of the law and of legal and governmental procedure. Only so could they utilize, or evade, it themselves. From there it would only be a step towards making or reforming the law.

Thus from 462 BC onwards, there was pressure for publication of the laws. The first proposal was associated with the name of a tribune, C. Terentilius Harsa (Livy 3.9.2) or C. Terentius (according to Dionysius 10.1.5). The name Terentilius is possibly Etruscan and, although not otherwise attested for such an early period, is not incredible. His proposal was for a commission of five with consular power to write down the laws. That at least is how Dionysius reports it. Livy, using a source which reflects the arguments about the extent of consular powers in the early part of the first century BC, varies it to a commission of five to write down the laws about consular powers. But Dionysius is clearly a more reliable authority here. The proposal dragged on for a number of years without being put into effect, until circumstances conspired to force it upon the government. The Roman historians attribute the pressure largely to a scandalous case in which Cincinnatus' son, K. Quinctius, was accused of assault by an ex-tribune, M. Volscius Fictor, and 'jumped' bail (Livy 3.11-24). The whole case, however, must be a fiction (as the name Volscius Fictor would indicate in itself), designed to provide a paradigm for the procedure of bail (*vadimonium*). It is riddled with unhistorical details, such as the financial sum involved (3,000 *asses*) and the subsequent withdrawal of Cincinnatus, and must be dismissed. The real pressure came from two very serious famines in 456 and 453 BC, coupled with the unremitting raids of the Sabines and Aequi. The final straw was a puzzling innovation attributed to the consuls Aternius and Tarpeius in 454 BC. Previously money had not been used as a means of exchange at Rome, except symbolically as a weight of metal in transactions such as *nexum*. Increasing contact with Greek cities may well have contributed to the decision to pass a law, which is cited by Cicero (*On the Republic* 2.60), Aulus Gellius (11.1.2) and Festus (268L.), establishing the equivalence 1 ox = 10 sheep = 100 lbs of bronze (*asses*). Since *asses* figure in the Twelve Tables, it must have been passed before 450 BC. As all societies have demonstrated, the institution of money as a means of exchange is liable to have a disruptive effect on the economy and to encourage debt. Although Attic coinage is later than Solon, the economic problems with which Solon had to deal were partly induced by the very recent invention of coinage in the Aegean world. The seriousness of the economic situation can be seen from the move by the plebeians to claim the Aventine as their own particular district.

It was in this climate that agreement was eventually reached to set up a commission of ten (Decemvirs) to regularize and publish the laws. The facts were much embellished in the course of time. The earliest version, probably derived from Polybius and by him from the first Roman historians, spoke of ten Commissioners 'to hold supreme power and to write the laws' (Cicero, *On the Republic* 2.61). The ten names, headed by Ap. Claudius and T. Minucius (Diodorus 12.23.1.; Livy and Dionysius give T. Genucius, a less likely figure), would have stood at the top of the original inscription setting out the laws. As the study of the Twelve Tables by scholars in the second and first centuries, such as Sex. Aelius Paetus and L. Aelius Stilo Praeconinus, revealed Greek elements in some of them, particularly the sumptuary laws, a direct connection with Greece was invented. Two alternatives were put forward. The annalists adopted the bold and flattering hypothesis that a Roman embassy (Sp. Postumius, A. Manlius and P. Sulpicius according to Livy 3.31.8) visited Athens to consult Solon's and other Greek laws. The antiquarian Varro identified a statue of Hermodorus in the Forum at Rome as portraying an exile from Ephesus who had fled to the West with the secrets of Ionian justice and expounded them to the Decemvirs (Pliny, *Natural History* 34.21). Neither alternative is in the least plausible, and the Greek elements come from the general contact with Greek thought, both direct and indirect (through Etruria), that had existed for 100 years.

The Decemvirs drew up Twelve Tables (or Schedules) of Law. The laws themselves do not survive, but they were regularly taught to children up to the end of the second century BC and were available for jurists to annotate for most of antiquity. They were cited either for linguistic peculiarities by grammarians and others or for fundamental principles of law by orators, politicians and lawyers. A few provisions were also of interest to historians (e.g. *conubium*). It is from such citations that we have to reconstruct their contents. The result appears as 'an unashamed mixture of private law, public law and administrative rules about public hygiene and safety'. Enough, however, can be recovered to give a fair idea of their scope, which can be summarized as follows.

1. Procedure for going to law and of summoning an opponent to appear in court (*manus iniectio*). The timing of court actions, and procedure for sureties for appearance (*vadimonium*).

2. Procedure about the deposit paid into court by parties to a dispute. Circumstances that justify postponement of an action, e.g. illness or unavoidable absence of one party. Penalties for default.

3. Action for debt. If judgement was brought against a party, he had thirty days to pay. In default after that period he was brought before the magistrate, and either produced a representative (*vindex*) who would be answerable for

twice the debt, or was bound over to the creditor for sixty days, after which time he could be sold into slavery across the Tiber, i.e. abroad (*trans Tiberim*: the attitude to Etruria is very notable), if the debt was still unpaid.

4. Provisions about the family, especially the rights of the head of the family (*patria potestas*), the safeguards for killing deformed children and regulations about divorce (the husband, in a formula, orders the wife to collect her belongings).

5. Provisions about women, children, lunatics in tutelage. Regulations about wills and intestacy.

6. Provisions about *nexum*. A wife passes into the possession (*manus*) of her husband unless she spends three nights away from home each year. Procedure for settling disputed cases of status (i.e. slave or free). Prohibitions against damaging other people's property. Foreigners do not have a good legal title.

7. Domestic regulations about boundaries, about the upkeep of roads and drains, about the ownership of acorns etc., that fall onto a neighbour's land.

8. Offences against other people and property. Magic spells and public demonstrations against individuals (*occeptare*) forbidden. Penalties for assault (*talio* ['an eye for an eye'], unless an agreed compromise is reached, in the case of *membrum ruptum*, 300 *asses* for *os fractum*), fire-raising, felling of other people's trees, stealing crops by night, theft by day or night. Interest to be no more than 100 per cent per annum. Safeguards for dependants – tutors punished doubly, a patron who defrauds his client is forfeit (*patronus si clienti fraudem fecerit, sacer esto*), false witnesses thrown from Tarpeian rock. Embargo on nocturnal assemblies. Regulations for clubs and assemblies.

9. No laws to be passed against individuals (*privilegia ne inroganto*). Capital cases involving citizens to be heard only before the main assembly, i.e. the comitia centuriata (*de capite civis nisi per maximum comitiatum ne ferunto*).

10. Regulations concerning the expense and manner of funerals. (These are largely modelled on Solonian precedents.)

11. A patrician may not marry a plebeian. A provision

about intercalation. Publication of the calendar.

12. Responsibility for crimes committed by slaves (*noxales actiones*).

It is likely that this summary gives the main scope of the Twelve Tables; but it leaves many unanswered questions of crucial importance.

1. The Tables are always spoken of by jurists as a single body of law, but all the historians consistently speak of the last two Tables being a later addition by a second commission of ten the following year (Cicero, *On the Republic* 2.63; Livy 3.37.4; Diodorus 12.26). Unfortunately the issue cannot be resolved archaeologically. The plural Tables (*Tabulae*) implies that they were originally written on separate wooden panels, and so the lawyer Pomponius in the second century AD asserted. At a later stage they were carved in bronze (Livy 3.57.10; Diodorus) and set up in the Forum. There is, there-fore, no means of knowing how many Tables there were to begin with. However, the Second Decemvirate is certainly a fiction since it contains several quite unhistorical names (e.g. M.' Rabuleius; cf. *rabula*, 'a pettifogger'). It was invented because the Decemvirate was regarded as a step forward in Rome's history, but one of the provisions of the Eleventh Table (namely that marriage was forbidden between plebeians and patricians) was deeply resented, as later events were to show. One solution was to assume that the last two Tables were added by wicked and unscrupulous men to the far-sighted and reforming achievement of their predecessors. I disregard the Second Decemvirate and the romances con-nected with it, such as Ap. Claudius and Virginia, entirely. They were devised to embroider the Twelve Tables and to simplify history.

2. Nevertheless, the dispute raises the difficult issue of how far the Decemvirs innovated or how far they merely codified existing practice which, until then, had been unpub-lished. Nothing can obviously be based on the legends of consulting Athenian law, and it is not easy to make judge-ments from the actual contents. Money fines had been in-troduced earlier: *Nexum* and most of the legal procedures such as *manus iniectio*, *vindicatio*, *vadimonium* appear to have been already in existence, but we have no 'cases' that we can

rely on. Three areas where innovation might be suspected prove curiously intractable.

a. The stringent provisions about funerals, including limitations on funeral veils, mourning dress, flute-players, gold-ornaments, give some temporal indications, because the datable tombs at Tarquinii between 530 and 470 BC show clear evidence of such extravagance, and it may be presumed to have existed under the Tarquins at Rome. But whether it was curtailed by the Decemvirs or, as one might more reasonably suppose, by the general economic necessity and the nationalistic revulsion against Veii and Etruria after 483 BC is much more difficult to decide.

b. The law forbidding marriage between patricians and plebeians was regarded by prejudiced historians as an innovation, but it is a question which, with our present knowledge, we cannot now solve because we do not know for certain the status of certain consular families which figure in the early Fasti, but which in later times emerge as plebeian (see p. 59). There is no indisputable example of a mixed marriage under the kings or the early Republic.

c. The law that no citizen should be put to death unless properly condemned by a court of law raises some obscure legal precedents. There was a settled tradition, invoked at the time of the assassination of Ti. Gracchus in 131 BC, that potential tyrants could be eliminated with impunity – they had stepped outside the constitution and therefore, if killed, were rightly killed – *iure caesi*. This was how the death of a demagogue, Sp. Maelius, in 440 BC, was justified by later historians (Livy 4.13). But the more relevant case was that of Sp. Cassius, who was alleged to have schemed for absolute power and to have been foiled and executed. Unfortunately the sources differ as to whether his death was the result of his outraged father exercising his paternal authority (*patria potestas*) or whether he was more constitutionally arraigned before *duoviri* (the responsible magistrates) for treason. Opinion is much divided. I am inclined to believe that he was summarily dealt with by his father, but even this is not proof that the Decemvirs were introducing an innovation. A whole generation had elapsed since the death of Sp. Cassius.

d. The least explicit evidence concerns what the Twelve

Tables laid down about the calendar and the Fasti. The Decemvirs are credited with a provision about intercalation, but that is as far as the sources go (Macrobius [fifth century AD], quoting [Sempronius] Tuditanus [first century BC] writes *de intercalando populum rogasse*). The standardization of a lunisolar calendar is, as has been argued, probably a Tarquinian innovation (see p. 41) and it will have involved some principle of intercalation. Whether the Decemvirs made public the mathematical calculations on which such intercalation was based or whether, in the light of the practical working of the calendar, they introduced some modification is quite unknown. The only other allusion is an aside by Cicero in a letter to his friend Atticus *to Att.* 6.1.8): 'you ask about Cn. Flavius. He certainly did not precede the Decemvirs, for he was *curule aedile*, which was a magistracy created a long time after the Decemvirs. What then did he achieve in publishing the Fasti? The view is that the relevant Table was at some date lost to view so that only a few should have access to the legal time-table.' Cicero implies that the Twelve Tables included the publication of the calendar, including such relevant facts as public festivals and days appropriate for legal or legislative business (see p. 42). Since the primary and traditional festivals (with the possible exception of the Lucaria) seem to belong to the epoch before 450 BC, it is not unreasonable to believe that the Decemvirs did make them publicly known once and for all. This in practice was a gesture that would have been of great value to the plebeians who were excluded from knowledge of religious mysteries. Once again, however, there is no conclusive proof of innovation.

The very thorough and perceptive studies by Franz Wieacker have established beyond doubt that the world of the Twelve Tables is the world of mid-fifth-century Rome. But it was no part of the Decemvirs' commission to reform the system. Their task was to clarify it and make it known. It was, therefore, only natural that when the plebeians discovered the facts, there should have been an instantaneous and devastating explosion.

The plebs seceded for the second time. By withdrawing themselves from Rome, they again brought life to a standstill and
forced some concessions. The historical sources attribute the
final breakdown to the tyrannical ambitions of Ap. Claudius
who threatened to retain his consular power as Decemvir
indefinitely and abused the very laws which he had framed
to get an innocent girl, Virginia, into his clutches. They
added another romantic myth, which was later to be much
invoked as an exemplary illustration of Roman heroism. L.
Siccius Dentatus, whose prowess had saved Rome on many
occasions, was callously sent to his death by Ap. Claudius.
Neither of these stories is likely to have any historical basis.
The true provocation was the sudden awareness, induced by
the publication of the Twelve Tables, of the constitutional
and legal disabilities of the plebeians. With the patriciate
now a fixed caste, plebeians could hope for no political ad-
vancement (either through obtaining office or through marriage) and they had little prospect of improving their disadvantaged position *vis-à-vis* the patricians with their patron-
client organization. Not for the last time knowledge of
the truth precipitated a revolution. It is more difficult to
establish what were the actual reforms introduced at this
time. The historians distinguish three main classes.

   1. Laws introduced by the popularist consuls L. Valerius
and M. Horatius in 449 BC as part of a package negotiation
bringing the secession to an end.
   2. Strengthening of the plebeian organization, especially
the tribunate.
   3. Subsequent measures aimed at amending those provisions of the Twelve Tables which particularly disadvantaged
the plebeians.
   At this range of time it is not easy to know whether
this tripartite division is historically correct; but careful
examination, which includes the rejection of some of the
ancient evidence, does result in a coherent picture which

broadly agrees with the traditional account, and which
answers to the social needs of the time in as far as we can
discern them.

1. Valerius and Horatius are credited with three laws
designed to improve the position of the plebeians. Each of
them is a subject of dispute.

The first was simply to enact that 'what the plebs decided in the tribal assembly should be binding on the whole
people', (Livy 3.55.1). The tribal assembly had been created
in 471 BC for the election of tribunes (see p. 109), but it was
quickly recognized as an efficient and representative assembly.
Nevertheless such sweeping powers are inconceivable at this
date. In any case it is known that the full status of laws was
not accorded to decisions of the tribal assembly (*plebiscita*)
until the Lex Hortensia of 287 BC. Either this Valerio-Horatian
law is a complete fiction or it was a much less far-reaching
measure than is reported by Livy. There are traces of
plebiscita appearing to have the force of law in the fourth
century (notably in 366 and 342 BC) and Livy mentions a
Lex Publilia of 339 BC (8.12.14) in almost exactly the same
terms as the Valerio-Horatian law. Scholars are divided in
their views. E. S. Staveley, attempting to reconcile all the
evidence, holds that the purpose of the Valerio-Horatian law
was to secure that if the Senate authorized the decision of
a tribal assembly it had the force of law, that in 339 BC
senatorial authorization was confined to laws introduced to
the tribal assembly by plebeian officials, whereas laws introduced by a consul to that assembly no longer required authorization, and that in 287 BC even this limitation was removed.
No mention of senatorial authorization, of course, occurs in
the terms of the supposed laws of either 449 or 339 BC and
we simply do not know at what stage consuls began to use
the tribal assembly for the dispatch of national (as opposed
to purely plebeian) business. The whole credibility of this
law must be judged in the general context of the legislation
attributed to Valerius and Horatius. There is certainly nothing
in the record of the next eighty years to suggest that such
a law was operative.

And the second law is clearly unhistorical. The terms of it
as given by Livy (3.55.3) are that 'no one should create

any magistracy without appeal (*provocatio*)'. *Provocatio* was
essentially the right of appeal from the summary jurisdiction
of a magistrate, in particular the consul, to the assembly of
the whole people. The basic question is how long established
this right was and at what level it operated. An older tradition than Livy's, preserved also by Cicero (*On the Republic*
2.53-4) and going back to Polybius and beyond, held that the
first consul, P. Valerius, in 509 BC, had introduced a bill that
'no magistrate should kill or chastise a Roman citizen in
defiance of an appeal to the people', and that this right had
existed even under the kings. Further 'the Twelve Tables in
several laws indicate that there was a similar right of appeal
from judgement and penalty. The tradition that the Decemvirs
who wrote the laws were appointed without appeal (*sine pro-
vocatione creatos*) is sufficient indication that the other magistrates were not without appeal. A consular law of L. Valerius
Potitus and M. Horatius Barbatus provided that no magistracy
should be created without appeal.' There is a deep ambiguity
in this evidence. It seems to imply two different things:
a. that the Decemvirate had absolute powers (i.e. there was no
appeal from its decisions) and that the Valerio-Horatian law
was designed to prevent the recurrence of such an autocratic
magistracy in future; and, by inference, b. that there was
appeal from the consul's summary jurisdiction (*coercitio*). The
first proposition is almost unbelievable. The Decemvirate was
a commission to frame laws and not an alternative form of
government. The belief in its absolute powers is part and
parcel of the growth of the myth about the tyrannical behaviour of Appius Claudius. The second proposition is more
difficult to assess. Cicero's evidence must be wrong on the
point of a magistrate's right to chastise without appeal, because there is no doubt that that restriction on a magistrate's
power was only introduced by one of three laws (all called
Leges Porciae) passed in the early second century. As to a
magistrate's power to execute, the right of appeal seems to be
incorporated in the Twelve Tables already under the provision 'that no one should be condemned on a capital charge
except before the main assembly' (see p. 121). When that
right was established is not clear, but, if the Twelve Tables
consolidated the law rather than made innovations, it is

likely to be long-standing, indeed to go back to the very institution of the dual consulship itself. What Cicero means
by writing that such a right of appeal was specified in
several laws of the Twelve Tables is uncertain in view of
our fragmentary knowledge of the contents of these laws,
but since the death-penalty was prescribed for numerous
offences, it could simply refer to these provisions. In any
event there does not seem to be room for a law such as
that ascribed to Valerius and Horatius. It was invented to support the democratic image of those two consuls. And if that
is the case, it clearly undermines the historicity of the first
law as well.

The third law, however, is more circumstantial. 'He who
should injure the tribunes of the plebs, the aediles, the
decemviral judges (*decemviris iudicibus*) should forfeit his
life to Jupiter and his possessions should be sold at the temple
of Ceres, Liber and Libera.' This law is much more plausible.
It is a formal restatement of the oath taken at the time of the
First Secession in 494 BC; and the proviso about the sale
of goods at the temple of Ceres is in accord both with the
character of that shrine (see p. 107) and with the well-established tradition that the goods of Sp. Cassius, who aimed at
a *coup d'état* in 486 BC (see p. 110), were dedicated likewise
to Ceres. An offering in her temple recording the dedication
was still accessible to the historian Piso (Pliny, *Natural History*
34.30). The only difficulty concerns the list of officials specified in the law. The tribunes already existed; aediles (the name
implies someone in charge of a temple or *aedes*) can safely be
presumed; but the decemviral judges (if they are a single
group, for the Latin could equally well be translated 'decemvirs and judges') are far harder to identify. Mommsen took
them to be a body known later as the *decemviri slitibus
iudicandis* who were concerned with deciding cases involving
the status of citizens and slaves, but it appears that this
body was only instituted after 242 BC. Therefore we are either
dealing with a primitive panel about which we know nothing
else or the law recorded by Livy contains an anachronism.
On balance the former is more likely. The plebs, in that case,
would have instituted not only ten tribunes but also ten
officials of their own to investigate certain judicial matters.

7. Ponte Sodo, Veii (PHOTO: PETER CLAYTON)

right: 8. The north-
east gateway, Veii
(PHOTO: PROFESSOR
H. H. SCULLARD)

below: 9.
Foundations of
the Portonaccio
Temple, Veii
(PHOTO: PROFESSOR
H. H. SCULLARD)

10. Early Roman Coinage

11. Funeral stele from Felsina
(PHOTO: PETER CLAYTON)

If this law is genuine it marks a significant stage in constitutional development. What had previously been a purely sectional organ became part of the recognized constitutional order.

The laws of Valerius and Horatius turn out therefore to offer very minimal reform. They merely strengthened and officially recognized some existing plebeian institutions.

2. Two other measures are associated with those years but are not specifically attributed to Valerius and Horatius. The first is the increase of the number of tribunes from four to ten. This is placed by Livy in 457 BC (3.30.7), six years *before* the Decemvirate. The date is not impossible, since we have seen above that there seems to be a panel of ten plebeian 'judges' already in existence by 449 BC, but it is more probable that the increase was inspired by a desire to match the number of Decemvirs. The confusion could have arisen from the simple fact that C. Horatius was consul in 457 BC and M. Horatius in 449 BC and that the change was dated to the wrong Horatius. In all events the total was ten from now on, and so it remained throughout Roman history. The second is more difficult. It was a matter of dispute whether a tribune could be re-elected for a further year or years. If he could not, what was to happen if enough candidates did not come forward or if the tribal assembly agreed on less than the full ten? This was a passionate issue in the second century when Tiberius Gracchus claimed the right to stand for re-election. Precedents were unearthed or invented, and a law, according to Appian (1.21), was in existence that if there was a deficiency of candidates the people could choose anyone (i.e. including previous tribunes who would normally be ineligible). This law (although it is not technically a law in that it only regulated the procedure for elections of tribunes of the plebs) is almost certainly the same as the proposal attributed to a tribune L. Trebonius in 448 BC (3.65.3): 'that the presiding officer at an election should continue to call upon the plebs to elect tribunes until he should effect the election of ten'. The inference to be drawn from this proposal is that until then vacancies were either left unfilled or were filled by co-option. And historians knew of another law which purported to say just that (3.64.10): 'if I shall call for your

votes for ten tribunes of the plebs; if for any reason you
shall elect today less than ten tribunes of the plebs, then
let those whom the elected tribunes co-opt as their colleagues
be as legally tribunes of the plebs as those whom you call
this day and have elected to that office'. But this law can be
shown on internal grounds to be a forgery, probably of the
second century BC, designed to provide a precedent for co-
option.

What emerges from this evidence and discussion is that
some procedural regularization of the election of tribunes was
made at this time. This is borne out by the fact that in 449 BC
the election of tribunes was presided over by the chief pontiff.
Livy identifies him as Q. Furius (3.54.5), Cicero as M. Papirius.
Papirius and Furius were colleagues in the consulship of 441
BC. Presumably the pontiff solemnized the election by taking
the auspices. It was another step in strengthening the plebeian
machinery. Once again it does not do anything about the
underlying tensions and divisions in the state.

3. The real issue was the disadvantaged status of plebeians,
and in particular their disqualification from marrying patricians or from holding offices confined to patricians. Whether
the consulship was such an office from the very beginning
or whether eligibility for it became increasingly restricted
in the first half-century of the Republic is an unresolved
question (see p. 80); but by 450 BC the prohibition was certainly absolute. The following years, however, saw two
initiatives for reform.

The first was a large-scale agitation led by a tribune, C.
Canuleius, in 445 BC to repeal the provision of the Twelve
Tables dealing with inter-marriage. His efforts were crowned
with success, despite the religious complications which such
a reform involved. The opposition argued that the auspices
(see p. 110) could only be held by patricians and that the
children of mixed marriages could not properly be ranked as
patricians. If mixed marriages became frequent, Rome would
ultimately be deprived of anyone to hold the auspices. The
argument, however, was fallacious because a basic principle
of Roman law was that the status of a child of a full legal
marriage (*iustae nuptiae*) was determined by his father's

status alone (*origo sequitur patrem*). The children of other irregular alliances were in a different situation: they took their mother's status (Gaius 1.76-96). If, therefore, inter-marriage between plebeians and patricians was recognized as *iustae nuptiae*, there would be no danger of the specifically patrician religious privileges dying out.

The historians tell an anecdote in connection with this heated debate. At Ardea there was a fatherless plebeian girl of great beauty who was courted by a plebeian and a 'patrician'. Her ambitious mother urged her to accept the patrician, whereas her guardians pressed her to accept the plebeian. The quarrel was referred to the magistrates who decided for the mother. This enraged the plebeians who abducted the girl. Civil war broke out, in the course of which the two sides turned to the Romans and the Volscians respectively for help. The international implications of this story will be considered later but the legal problems have been the subject of much dispute in recent years. I doubt whether any Ardeate law or any Ardeate legend of this kind can have survived from the fifth century, and therefore believe that the episode is designed to throw into relief the essentially *Roman* issue: could or should a plebeian marry a patrician? Two leading scholars of Roman law in Italy and England, Professors Volterra and Daube, have challenged this, largely on the ground that, if the story had been invented to illustrate the Roman debate on inter-marriage, it should have involved a patrician girl and a plebeian suitor. But what was really at stake was whether the patrician status would be lost if a patrician *man* married beneath him, because only in that way would the religious prerogatives be eliminated.

The Lex Canuleia went some way to solving the social tensions between plebeians and patricians. The political tensions, however, remained. In 444 BC instead of the usual election of two consuls it was decided to elect a college of 'military tribunes with consular power'. Such colleges were elected in several of the years between 444 and 367 BC and the number of tribunes each year grew steadily from three to six. There are some uncertainties and contradictions in the sources (e.g. for 434 Diodorus gives a list of three tribunes whereas the sources used by Livy gave two consuls, although there was further doubt about their identity) but the pattern is clear

3   444, 438, 434(?), 433, 432, 422, 418, 408
4   426, 425, 424, 420, 419, 417, 416, 415, 414, 407, 406
6   405, 404, 403(?), 402, 401, 400, 399, 398, 397, 396, 395, 394, 391, 390 . . .

The original motive for the change to tribunes is not recorded, but there were explanations current in later antiquity (Livy 4.7.1). A purely military view held that Rome's increasing commitments and the threat of war on several fronts required more than two supreme commanders. Others held that the motive was political: a plebeian demand for the right to hold one of the consulships was outflanked by creating a new office for which plebeians were eligible but which would not infringe the patrician religious monopoly of the consulship. The subject has been much canvassed by modern scholars. The military explanation derives considerable support from the very fact of their name: they were tribunes of the *soldiers*, and since it seems that a tribune was in charge of 1,000 soldiers (see p. 101) the increase in the number of tribunes corresponds to the increasing size of the levy (*legio*), until by 405 BC the legions had been stabilized as 6,000 men with six tribunes, just as in 311 BC, if the text of Livy is correctly emended (9.30.3), a law was passed insisting on the democratic election to the six tribunates of each of the four legions. The political explanation is at first suspect. Livy can be shown to have taken it from the politically tendentious historian, C. Licinius Macer (see p. 120), and significantly the first plebeian said by him to have been elected was a P. Licinius (5.12.9). However, the demise of the military tribunes coincides with a law in 366 BC which *did* open the consulship to plebeians. Secondly, as far as can be seen, no military tribune held a triumph, the crowning glory of military success (Zonaras 7.18). Thirdly, as a matter of historical fact, the years when there were military tribunes were not the years of maximum military activity; and when there was a crisis, as in 396 BC with the capture of Veii, or in 390 BC with the defeat by the Gauls, or, to a lesser extent, in 418 BC, a dictator was appointed as generalissimo. Most of the fighting was otherwise done in the years when there were consuls. Now the main function of the consuls was bound to be a military one. Therefore it may well be that the true explanation is a compromise. When serious military activity was not anticipated, the tribunes of the levy were designated as the eponymous magistrates in order to allow plebeians the opportunity of holding supreme power, but when war was expected the state reverted to patrician consuls who alone had the religious privilege of ascertaining the will of the gods through the auspices, and the right to triumph. Sometimes it was not possible to predict what the year would hold in store, and changes had to be made in the course of it to meet emergencies.

This solution leaves one problem unresolved. The supreme magistrate did have other than military responsibilities. He had powers of summary jurisdiction and he had the duty of summoning and presiding over the centuriate assembly. The judicial powers could presumably have been conferred on military tribunes by a legislative decision: this is what 'tribunes of the soldiers *with consular power*' would mean. But an assembly required divine approval, sought through the auspices. The answer to this problem is not known: it may have been laid down that at least one of the tribunes should always be a patrician who could exercise this power. No year seems to have been without a patrician tribune, even if only one.

There was, however, another religious and administrative duty which the consuls must have performed up till this time. In order to form the levy, it was necessary to have a register of eligible men of the right age and with the right financial qualification – the pool from which the fighting centuries were drawn. Such a register, the *classis*, needed periodic revision. Furthermore, a fighting force was an uncomfortable thing from a religious point of view. It required special rituals to free it from the taint of blood-guilt before it could be reincorporated in the community. At Rome the people, meeting as the centuriate assembly whose nature and purpose were primarily military, always met *outside* the proper boundaries of the city. In the later Republic a provincial governor had to drop his command before he was allowed to enter the city. Servius Tullius is credited with being the first person to have compiled the register or census and to have conducted the religious rituals in connection with the establishment of the centuriate body or potential army. The Latin phrase for this ritual, *lustrum condere*, is obscure and its meaning much disputed. *Lustrum* should be derived from a root which means 'to loose' and, therefore, to signify 'that which looses' (i.e. frees from pollution). *Condere*, which in classical Latin means 'to store, to found' is formed from a root which should give the basic meaning 'to put together'. The question is what was the essence of the ritual, what was 'put together as a purifying element'. The practice of other states such as Iguvium, whose ceremonies are preserved in a series of inscriptions, suggests that it may have been the ritual kindling of fire, the most drastic of purifiers.

However that may be, it was a duty of prime religious significance performed first by the kings, by virtue of their supreme and sacral power and subsequently by the consuls who inherited their religious prerogative. When, however, the chief magistracy was opened to people who did not enjoy the religious privilege of the patricians it was necessary to create special magistrates to discharge it. These were the censors, whose creation is said by the historians to have coincided with the innovation of the military tribunes in 444 BC (Livy 4.8.2). The meaning of the word *censor* is also in doubt, but philologically it should be an agent noun from a root meaning 'to light a fire' (cf. *incendo*); and this squares with what seems to have been the central act in the religious ceremony which accompanied the compiling of the military register. Later derivatives, such as *census*, and *censeo*, 'I enumerate or adjudicate', will be derived from what the censors actually did. The censors made a periodic assessment of the Roman people (it became standardized at every five years) which they concluded by purifying the assembly through a ceremony in which sacrificial victims (a pig, a sheep and a bull) were led three times round the company, before being sacrificed, and the sacred fire was solemnly rekindled as an act of purification.

That there was an increase in military activity is obvious, not only from the growing number of military tribunes over the years, but also from the actual accounts of warfare which are preserved and which will be analysed in the next chapter. Having a special magistracy to supervise the census will have led to much greater efficiency in the assessment and selection of the *classis*, because the introduction of bronze (*aes*) as a form of currency, which was regularized for fines by the Lex Aternia Tarpeia and incorporated in the Twelve Tables, added to the complication of assessing wealth. When it could be done simply by counting cattle or measuring land few problems were posed; but when this had to be converted into terms of a conventional means of exchange the work would have been doubled. Although Greek cities had by now fine coinages of their own, the Romans were slow to adopt a similar standard. The currency of the mid-fifth century consisted of rough lumps of bronze without uniform shape or size (*aes rude*) whose value was determined purely by weight. This was refined at a later date (see p. 152) into recognizable units of a more or less uniform weight and identified by stamps (*aes signatum*). The first individual coins (*aes grave*) do not appear before the end of the fourth century (see Plates 10 and 11). The delay in their appearance is no doubt due to the economic collapse that followed on the sack of Rome by the Gauls and the slow recovery thereafter. In the same way the actual management of public finances, particularly in the military field, became more intricate, and international negotiations, for instance over the purchase of corn, necessitated some specialist competence. Tacitus (*Annals* 11.22), discussing the quaestorship, the annual junior magistracy concerned with finance, says that it was first established in 446 BC when two quaestors were appointed 'to be attached to the War Department'. The word quaestor means 'investigator' and there had been earlier quaestors, appointed presumably *ad hoc*, to investigate cases of homicide, who are referred to in the Twelve Tables. The permanent magistracy, however, was an innovation. Its purpose is clear although we know nothing about the social qualifications required by candidates. If they had to be patrician, it will have been in part a move by the patricians to maintain their monopoly of government, even

after they had conceded the institution of the military tribunate with consular power. The quaestors' job was mainly concerned with supplies, stores and finance. Its importance is
shown by the fact that within a generation the number of
quaestors was doubled from two to four (see p. 151).

When, therefore, the reforms of the 440s are reviewed, it
transpires that they probably did little more than consolidate
the power of the plebeian tribunes, remove certain grievances
of the plebs, and improve the administrative efficiency of the
Roman military machine. The fundamental issues were not
tackled, and persisted in different ways to cloud the politics
of the next two centuries. Nor were the economic conditions
significantly eased, and these were to provoke a succession
of troubles in the next generation.

National difficulties can sometimes divide and sometimes unite a country. It depends to a large extent on the mood of the people. Although it is difficult to reconstruct the history of the generation after the Decemvirate, we know enough to realize that it was a time of great economic distress and, equally, of great political bitterness.

The economic indications are derived partly from the historical records and partly from archaeological inferences. In the first place there is a strong tradition of major corn-shortages in 440 when corn had to be imported from Etruria, 437, 433, when requests for help were made to coastal Etruscan cities, Cumae and Sicily, and 411, when again Etruria, Cumae and Sicily were turned to for help with varying degrees of response. The immediate cause must have been crop-failure, which will not have been helped by the regular succession of plagues which attacked the population during those years (437, 436, 435, 433, 432, 431, 428, 412, 411) and are said to have struck the farming community in particular (Livy 4.25.4). The medical nature of those illnesses cannot be now recovered, but their prevalence is borne out by the fact that in 433 a temple to Apollo, the god of healing, was vowed, and was dedicated two years later. Cults reflect the needs of the moment and the memory of the establishment of the cult of Apollo is a detail that will have been preserved quite independently of the annalistic notices about plagues and famines.

Confirmation of this picture can be gained from archaeology. Trade with Etruria seems to have closed down in the second half of the century. Imported Attic pottery and Etruscan terra-cottas cease after 450 BC. Nor is there any evidence for Roman or Latin influences in the Etruscan markets of the period. One further detail may be relevant. Under the year 400 BC Livy mentions that several starving and desperate plebeians covered their heads, jumped into the Tiber and drowned themselves (4.12.11). Now a notice in the scholar Festus (66L.)

refers to 'off-the-bridge old men, who were thrown from the bridge when they reached the age of 60'. This barbaric practice has been rejected by some scholars who hold that it is no more than a mistaken explanation of another religious ceremony when bundles of used reeds, working into human shape, were each year carried in procession and finally thrown into the Tiber. The bundles were called Argei – Argive men (?). No ancient sources, however, connect the two rituals and one must never play down the latent violence and cruelty at Rome. Defaulting debtors could, like Antonio be cut in pieces, according to the Twelve Tables, and human sacrifice survived until the third century. The drowning plebeians may be a genuine glimpse of a despairing community.

It is against this background that a second feature needs to be viewed. Livy and Dionysius of Halicarnassus both mention as one of the persistent political pressures of the time the demand by the plebs to be allocated land outside Rome on which to live and farm. These abortive agrarian laws are a recurring theme. Livy, for example, records such agitation under the years 441, 424, 421, 420, 416, 414, 410. It is not easy to know what to make of this. In the first place it would be surprising if *abortive* laws were recorded in the Annales. Secondly, there is no doubt that much of the political colouring, as it is painted by Livy, is toned and blended by the much later arguments over the Gracchan agrarian legislation : history was rewritten to provide a precedent for the contemporary events of the Gracchi. Thirdly, Livy gives the impression of enormous areas of public land being exploited by a few monopolistic land-owners, and that, given the actual circumstances of fifth-century Latium, is a blatant anachronism and exaggeration. Nevertheless, we can hardly dismiss the tradition entirely. People were short of food, and they may well have felt that they could create a better livelihood for themselves in a Latin village than they could at Rome, or on Roman land where patrician clients got first preference. The problem was probably not one of pure patrician obstinacy but of practical politics. Latium too was hard-pressed : there was very little land available, and Rome's allies had first claim on what there was.

To the south the Volscians were now well established and

much of the old Roman sphere of influence – Circeii and Terracina – was lost for good. Even nearer home, the city of Ardea, which had earlier been firmly in Rome's orbit during the late sixth century, was a subject of keen dispute. Some time about 450 BC or earlier Ardea fell to the Volscians. Her geographical position was too important for the Latins to overlook, because it opened the way to the rest of the Latin plain up to the River Tiber. A concerted effort was made by Rome and her allies which resulted in the recapture of the site and its repopulation by a Latin colony under Roman supervision in 442 BC (Livy 4.11.5; Diodorus 12.34.5). But there was little spare land at Ardea for disenchanted Roman plebeians to occupy.

Nor was the situation any easier to the east. Here the key was the Alban Hills. If once the Volscians or the Aequi could break through that gateway, they would overrun Latium. The fight, therefore, was for the command of the Alban Hills and the main road (the Via Latina) that ran through them. The places mentioned in the succession of campaigns which ranged between 431 and 409 BC can for the most part be identified and a glance at the map shows their strategic importance – Labici which defected in 419 BC and was recaptured the following year, Bola which changed hands in 415 and 414 BC, the citadel of Carventum, near Tusculum, perhaps Mte Fiore, which was the scene of desperate fighting in 410 BC and 409 BC, Verrugo 'the wart', probably Maschia d'Ariano guarding the easterly gap in the Alban Hills, which the Romans recaptured in 409 BC only to lose again two years later. These wars are detailed and plausible. Livy (4.28.3) even recalls the name of one of the enemy commanders, Vettius Messius, which reflects the title of the chief magistrate of the Oscan people, meddix, and so is likely to preserve something of genuine tradition. The wars were long drawn-out and messy. They could not be resolved by a single, decisive battle. They consisted of minor skirmishes, persistent infiltration and guerrilla operations. The Romans required a large army to deal with a relatively small number of mobile aggressors, so that they quickly saw the need to enlist the services of the local population to act partly as a buffer-state and partly as a first line of defence. They were fortunate

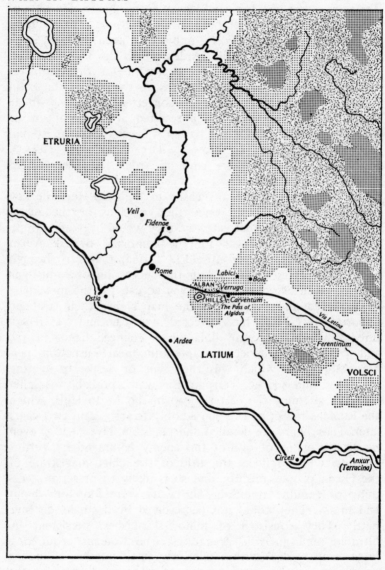

enough to win over a local tribe, the Hernici, who served them with courage and loyalty but who also exacted their reward. When the land and town of Ferentinum were captured from the Volscians in 413 BC, they were handed over as compensation to the Hernici – which became yet another source of grievance for the unemployed and hungry proletariat at Rome.

For over twenty years the Romans held their own against the Volscians. The cost of these wars was heavy. The need to maintain what was virtually a standing army of some 4,000 men made severe demands on the economy, and the irregular nature of the fighting led to the destruction of crops and the deterioration of the land. But there was an even more serious threat to Rome's trade. Fidenae, the Etruscan outpost on the Roman side of the Tiber commanding the Via Salaria, which must have passed under Roman control in the early part of the century (see p. 92), decided to revolt, and turned for help to the king of Veii, Lars Tolumnius. Neither the cause nor the precise date of the revolt is known (Livy puts it, reasonably enough, in 438 BC) but the event is likely to be linked with the tensions which Veii herself was experiencing as a result of the same economic pressures that were depressing all central Italy. The revolt sparked off a major crisis, intensified by the murder of four Roman ambassadors at the Veientane court. Rome had to resort to force and in the course of military operations a Roman commander, A. Cornelius Cossus, killed his opposing general and won, for only the second time in history, the *spolia opima* (see p. 38). This feat was remembered and handed down, but there may also have been more circumstantial evidence. The emperor Augustus, some time about 29 BC, claimed to have inspected the actual linen corselet dedicated by Cossus in the temple of Jupiter Feretrius and to have seen an inscription on it which recorded that Cossus was consul when he won the *spolia* (Livy 4.20.5-9). It is not inconceivable that the corslet should have survived even though the temple had been in a ruinous state for some years, but Augustus' statement is not beyond suspicion, since the official title of the supreme magistrate should at this date have been *praetor*. Nor could Augustus have misunderstood or misread the cognomen *Cossus* because such names were not officially written at this date. Augustus probably had a political motive in reading the inscription, whatever it was, as he did, in that he disallowed a claim by M. Licinius Crassus in 29 BC to be awarded the *spolia opima* on the grounds that he was only a proconsul and not a full consul. In any case it may well have been 'restored' and modernized in the four hundred years since its dedication.

The corselet, however, is tangible proof of the action against Fidenae. It is also relevant to the question of date. If Cossus was consul, then a crucial battle must have been fought in 428 BC when he was consul with T. Quinctius. The sources do indeed speak of trouble at Fidenae that year which led to a judicial enquiry into the movements of certain suspected citizens of Fidenae who were subsequently deported to Ostia, but they do not speak of a major encounter which they attribute instead to 437 or to 426. In both of these years Mam. Aemilius is credited with a dictatorship and a successful attack on Fidenae. Aemilius' part in the reduction of Fidenae was also recorded by the Triumphal Records of 437 BC, but in that year Cossus held no official position at all. He would in fact have been too young, and Livy mentions him as serving as a junior officer in the army under Aemilius. That leaves 426 BC when he was consular tribune and also appointed by Aemilius as his Master of Horse. Certainty is impossible. Cossus' exploit was obviously an independently remembered thing. All that can plausibly be conjectured is that for twelve years Rome was not able to secure Fidenae's allegiance decisively. It required several interventions and several battles before the position was thoroughly stabilized. Fidenae possessed a strong natural site which would have been difficult to capture without overwhelming numbers and competent siege-machinery. When it did eventually succumb, the Romans strengthened their control over it by sending a detachment of colonists and assigning them some nearby land. It is also to be noted that some leading Roman citizens, who bore the cognomen *Fidenas*, such as L. Sergius (consul in 437) and Q. Servilius, and whose families, therefore, presumably originated from Fidenae, are reported to have taken an active role in dealings with the town, no doubt in an attempt to reassert their influence over their former fellow-countrymen.

Although we cannot recover in detail the course of relations between Rome and Fidenae over these years, we can have confidence in the general picture. Indeed it receives further confirmation from three other sources. Inscriptions from Veii preserve the name of Tulumne as one of the leading families of the city in the sixth century, while Cicero mentions that a statue-group survived to his day commemorating 'Tullus Cluilius, L. Roscius, Sp. Nautius and C. Fulcinius who were killed by the king of Veii' (*Philippic* 9.4-5). There is no reason to doubt the authenticity of such an inscribed statue- group, and the names of Cluilius and Nautius belong to families which were active in the fifth century. Finally a note in Livy (4.34.6) refers to an engagement at Fidenae in 426 by the *classis*. In classical Latin this would normally denote the fleet, and so Livy apologetically assumed it to mean; but, of course, Rome had no fleet of consequence at this date, and even if it had, a naval battle on the Tiber off Fidenae would be distinctly bizarre. In fact the note must refer to the mobilization of the centuriate army (the eligible class as opposed to those below the class, *infra classem*; see p. 46) and its involvement at Fidenae. The obscurity and accuracy of the note (for there was as yet only one eligible class) suggest that it must have been derived from a contemporary record.

The defection of Fidenae not only threatened Rome's trade up the Tiber. It also brought Rome into serious confrontation with Veii once more and imposed a further military burden on the community. The hardship caused by continuous warfare on three fronts and by recession was bound to affect popular morale. There is a continuing tradition, reported by Livy, of resistance by the tribunes of the plebs to the annual military levy, which, if there is any truth in it – and it is not a fact which one would naturally expect to find its way into the pontifical record – suggests widespread discontent and disquiet. Fortunately this rather dubious tradition does not have to be relied upon, because there are two well-attested stories which point to exactly the same conclusion, and mirror a community embittered by economic distress and riven by political discord.

The first, traditionally dated to 441-40, became part of the stock-in-trade of the late Republic politicians. A knight, Sp. Maelius, used his private contacts and resources in order to import a substantial quantity of corn from Etruria, which he sold at competitive prices or even gave away to the plebs, and thereby acquired a potent, if temporary, popularity. It was a time of famine, and the state had already appointed a prefect, L. Minucius, to coordinate the public corn-supply. Maelius' head was turned by his success, and he set on foot a scheme to seize supreme power, which Minucius duly heard of and reported to the Senate. The Senate encouraged a thug, C. Servilius Ahala, to assassinate Maelius – or at least condoned his action. This certainly is the earliest version of the story and implies a plausible view of the rough justice of fifth-century politics. It was later 'legitimized' by historians reacting to the summary violence of the Gracchan age. C. Servilius was no longer classed as a private person. A state of emergency had been declared, and Servilius had been appointed Master of Horse under the dictator L. Quinctius Cincinnatus, whose earlier career had already become legendary (see p. 111). He had, according to this version, legal powers to carry out his rough justice. The bare bones of the story belong to the basic fabric of oral tradition in Roman history, even though there are some disconcerting elements. There was an area called the Aequimaelium at the south-east corner of the Capitol whose name was explained by ancient scholars, with some improbability, as being where Maelius' house was levelled after his assassination. Still worse, the Aequimaelium was located near a statue column associated with the family of the Minucii: the column figures on coins minted by Minucii in the period 140-103 BC, and was said by the historian Piso to have been erected in honour of this L. Minucius (Pliny, *Natural History* 18.15). Furthermore there was a Minucian Portico (Porticus Minucia) which was a centre of the grain market, situated in the south-east corner of the city. However, neither the statue-column nor the Portico can be earlier than the third century on archaeological grounds; this casts doubt on the role of L. Minucius in 441 as a public servant of the state in charge of the corn supply. Such scepticism, however, is perhaps too thorough-going. Livy records that an early list of magistrates written on linen (*libri lintei*) recorded Minucius' name as prefect this year. It is immaterial whether a specific responsibility for corn (*praefectus annonae*) or a more general responsibility for the city (*praefectus urbi*) was intended. These linen records are among the earliest attested documents for Roman magistrates and were stored in the temple of Moneta, dedicated in 344 BC. They are, therefore, among our most original and reliable sources. Minucius had a public position at Rome, and Maelius was assassinated. As in the earlier case of Sp. Cassius, a potentially revolutionary situation is revealed, where an individual can win substantial support for himself by exploiting the economic distress and the political dissatisfaction.

The leading families at this juncture of Roman history seem to have been the Postumii and the Sempronii, both probably of Etruscan origin but by now thoroughly Romanized. The Sempronii were, in later generations, a plebeian family but their appearance in the consular Fasti of the fifth century is an indication that they must have been patrician then. The Postumii were certainly patrician, and there survived a memory that they had championed the patrician cause in league with the Sempronii (Dionysius 10.41.5). They acquired something of a monopoly of the chief magistracies: A. Sempronius Atratinus, the first consular tribune in 444 BC and perhaps a brother L. Sempronius Atratinus consul in the same year; in the next generation, A. Sempronius Atratinus consul in 428, consular tribune in 425, 420, 416 and his brother, C. Sempronius Atratinus consul in 423: Sp. Postumius Albus consular tribune in 432, A. Postumius Tubertus dictator in 431, M. Postumius, consular tribune in 426, M. Postumius Regillensis, consular tribune in 414 BC. But their success was not commensurate with their distinction.

The war with Fidenae dragged on; the wars against the Volscians were perennial and inconclusive. The awareness of military shortcomings is seen in the decisions taken in 421 to raise the number of quaestors, the administrative officials, from two to four and in 409 to elect plebeians as quaestors, thereby ensuring the widest possible field of choice. Some hints of the criticism that was felt against the government can be pieced together. In 431 A. Postumius won a

hard-fought victory against the Volscians under Vettius
Messius at Algidus, the strategic pass of the Alban Hills. A
legend survived that he had executed his own son for leaving his place in the battle, as a later general T. Manlius
Torquatus was to do in 347 BC. The proverb 'Postumian
discipline' was handed down (Aul. Gell. 1.13). In hoplite fighting, precise discipline was essential to preserve the cohesion
of the phalanx, and this may be what lies behind the story.
But, in any case, it suggests ruthless measures and uncertain
morale. M. Postumius was defeated at Veii in 426 and C.
Sempronius at Verrugo in 423, when the army was only
saved by the efforts of subordinate commanders. Ten years
of dissatisfaction erupted into a series of personal attacks on
the two families. The story has obviously been written up but
there is enough solid evidence to reconstruct the facts. Livy
mentions four plebeians, Sex. Tempanius, M. Asellius, T.
Antistius and (?) Sp. Pullius, as having acted with great
presence of mind as non-commissioned officers at Verrugo.
Three years later C. Sempronius, the unlucky commander on
that occasion, was finally convicted and fined. Livy names
the ringleaders against him as three tribunes of the plebs,
Antistius, Sex. Pullius (?; the name is corrupt) and M. Canuleius. It looks as if the same individuals are involved, but that
M. Canuleius has been substituted for M. Asellius because
of the fame of the earlier Canuleius (see p. 130). This is corroborated by a fragmentary inscription (dating from the early
imperial age but probably a reconstruction of an earlier monument) which names Ti. Antistius, son of Ti. Antistius, as having
dedicated or built something in the consular tribunate of
[Me]nenius Agrippa and Lucretius T[ricipitinus] – that is in
the year 419 BC. The most likely hypothesis is that the courage
of the four men and their prosecution of C. Sempronius
was commemorated in an inscription, just as the death of
the four ambassadors at Veii was similarly commemorated.
Further manifestations of this hostility are the prosecution,
also in 420, of Postumia, a Vestal Virgin, for indecorous
behaviour – a fact that will certainly have been noted in the
pontifical records – and the successful prosecution of her
brother, M. Postumius, for his failure at Veii. Finally M.
Postumius Regillensis in 415 BC was stoned by his own troops

after upbraiding them for their failure against the Aequi at Bolae.

The period ends on a note of profound gloom, lightened only by the recovery of Fidenae and by the fact that the Volscians were still being held at bay. The army had displayed over the thirty years weaknesses of technique, morale and leadership, and the people of Rome, harassed by sickness, poverty and military failure, were divided and discontented. It was at this juncture that the most serious threat to Rome's existence arose. Veii challenged Rome, and for a number of years (traditionally ten but the war acquired the epic proportions of a Trojan War at an early stage), Rome was engaged in a life and death struggle. It emerged from that struggle, under the inspiration of one man, M. Furius Camillus, with a much improved army and a stronger sense of corporate unity, which, though it left the main political problems unresolved, held out the prospect of compromise and progress in the future.

Rome's first brush with Veii had ended in stalemate. The Romans had indeed lost decisively at Cremera but Veii seems to have made no attempt to follow up the victory. Livy speaks of a forty-year non-aggression pact signed in 474 BC (see p. 116) but this is likely to be a fiction based only on the fact that Veii was not engaged in hostilities against Rome for some forty years. During that space of time things had changed. The Romans had become more conscious of their own national identity and thought of themselves less as part of the Etruscan cultural world. The natural rivalry between the two cities was also intensified by economic necessity. There were three main factors. Firstly, much of Rome's trade depended on salt, but Veii also had saltbeds, on the right bank of the mouth of the Tiber; and a road led directly to them from Veii. The markets for salt were the great inland cities, Clusium, Arretium and so on, and one can infer Roman commercial links with Clusium not only from Porsenna's intervention at Rome (see p. 88) but from the fact that the people of Clusium turned for help to Rome, when threatened by the Gauls in the 390s, and negotiations were conducted with a delegation of the Fabian family, whose Etruscan contacts have already been discussed (see 110). Rome and Veii were competing for the same markets and those markets were themselves menaced by the Celts (see p. 160). Secondly, Veii, like Rome, was an important entrepôt for trade between Etruria and the rich markets of southern Italy, commanding, as it did, vital Tiber crossings and the access to the through route to Campania. Much of this traffic, however, had dried up as the result of the Etruscan losses in Campania in 474 and the consequent advance of the Samnites. What trade continued with the Greek cities probably went by sea now, and the land-route itself was made unhealthy by the continuous operations of the Aequi and Volscians.

Veii was hit commercially, and this is reflected in the marked deterioration of her products seen both from the

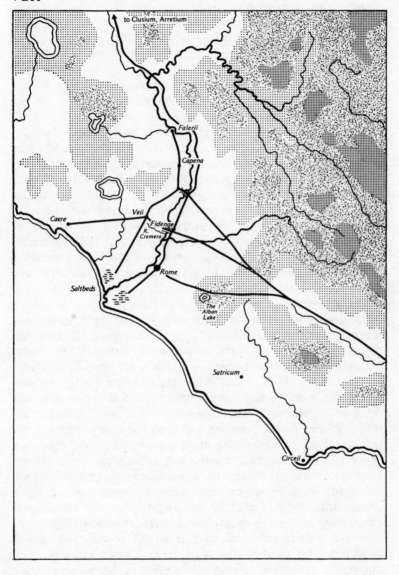

to Clusium, Arretium

Falerii

Capena

Caere

Veii

Fidenae
R.
Cremera

Saltbeds

Rome

The
Alban
Lake

Satricum

Circeii

site of the city and from the great cemeteries around it. Thirdly, Veii possessed a very large territory, much larger, proportionately, than Rome; and, if one of the sources of discontent at Rome was shortage of land for arable or pastoral purposes, Veii's broad acres must have attracted jealous eyes from across the Tiber.

The defection of Fidenae was a provocative action, but it did not bring Rome and Veii into serious conflict at the time. Rome had enough on her hands without openly challenging Veii, and Veii also seems to have had political troubles. In 437 BC it was ruled by a king, Lars Tolumnius. At some stage he or his dynasty was overthrown, because under the year 403 BC Livy reports (5.1.2) that the Veientes 'bored with the annual competition for election, decided to appoint a king', implying that a republican magistracy had been in existence for a number of years. No source recounts how the king had fallen on the first occasion; but it is legitimate to infer some political tensions at Veii during the generation from 436-406, which may have accounted for Veii's relative quiescence.

The ancient sources blame the outbreak of war on Veii's intransigence – a specious grievance backed by threats and ultimatums. This very fact is in itself suspicious. Roman historians are always at pains to put Rome firmly in the right, irrespective of the circumstances. All wars waged by Rome are just wars. It is more likely that border hostilities simmered for a few years until Rome took a decisive step and resolved to eliminate the menace of Veii once and for all. It is that step which provides a clue to the true chronology of the war and its underlying motivation. The exact dates are beyond recall: the traditional dates of 406-396 are certainly inaccurate; Veii is likely to have fallen, in historical fact, about 392 BC, after six or seven years of intermittent fighting culminating in a full-scale onslaught. But the traditional chronology will serve as a close enough approximation.

If Veii was to be eliminated, it would require not only a large army by itself (quite apart from Rome's military commitments on other fronts). It needed a permanent army capable of maintaining a lengthy siege, and an army with fast communications and the flexibility which only an effective cavalry can provide. In 405 (traditional date), for the first time, six consular tribunes were elected which presupposes an army of 6,000 – a third as large again as any previous levy. This increase was accompanied by further significant innovations. Two years later M. Furius Camillus and M. Postumius Albinus were censors (so at least all the sources agree, except for Livy who assumes an impossible college of no less than eight consular tribunes). Postumius had been consular tribune in 426 but Camillus was a portent. The Furii were an old family, who dated back to the Etruscan kingdom and who had provided several consuls and consular tribunes during the fifth century. Camillus' brother was consul in 413 BC. But Camillus had not held the highest offices of state before he was elected censor – an unparalleled situation. The cognomen *Camillus* was the title of a patrician boy employed in religious duties, and there is no reason to doubt that such had been his upbringing. But he must have had other qualities, especially military originality of a high order, to have been selected for the principal military and administrative office in the state as a young and inexperienced man. The difficulty with Camillus is that his personality became overlaid with accretions of legend as time progressed. In particular his career was remoulded by historians to provide precedents for Scipio Africanus, Sulla and Julius Caesar. One has, therefore, to strip away all the trappings and try to recover the essential and authentic facts.

What emerges is that the period of Camillus' censorship witnessed not only the critical decision to destroy Veii but a number of military reforms which were necessary if that decision was to be successfully executed. The main reforms are four:

1.   The increase of the army to 6,000 probably meant that 2,000 men below the financial requirement of the *classis* were called up, since the number of centuries of *iuniores* (active soldiers) in the *classis*, or first class, remained forty. They were less well armed – Livy, for instance, says that they were not equipped with a breast-plate – and served in second-line duties.

2.   Some reform of the cavalry was undertaken. Livy alleges

that volunteers from the equestrian order offered to serve as cavalry with their own horses (5.7.4-13) but at the same time were paid for their services. It is extremely difficult to reconstruct what actually occurred. The emphasis of the early fifth-century army was entirely on infantry (see p. 46); and it may well be that in addition to the old six centuries of cavalry (Sex Suffragia) which had existed since regal times, a further twelve centuries were now instituted, bringing the cavalry establishment up to 1,800. The figure of eighteen cavalry centuries became conventional in historical times. The cost of this was met by two taxes – the *aes equestre* and *aes hordearium* (fodder tax) – traditionally levied by Servius Tullius on orphans and widows (Livy 1.43.9 : Cicero, *On the Republic* 2.36) but more plausibly attributed to Camillus and his fellow-censor of 403 BC by Plutarch (*Life of Camillus* 2; cf. Valerius Maximus 2-9.1). In other words, extra cavalry were recruited who were paid for by the state – they had a 'public horse' – rather than financing themselves, as had been the case before.

3. Diodorus (14.16.5) and Livy (4.59.11) both state that early in the war with Veii the soldiers were paid for the first time in history on a regular basis. Although payment does not seem to have been normal until at least the third century, the special circumstances of an all-year siege may easily have inspired special measures. The men were, after all, being deprived of the chances of earning a livelihood in other ways, and financial compensation was essential, if morale, which had been suspect in earlier years, was to be maintained.

4. Less certainly, some changes in armour may have been made at this time. At some point the older hoplite phalanx which relied on a small shield (*clipeus*), a thrusting spear and a highly disciplined close-formation (see p. 45) gave place to a more flexible organization in which the chief weapons were larger shields, swords and throwing spears (*pila*). This was the organization that lasted down until the second century BC. Livy (8.8) says that this occurred after the troops began to be paid, and Plutarch, in his *Life of Camillus*, attributes what may amount to the same reform to Camillus. Neither passage is free from difficulty and neither may be based on any authentic evidence but it is significant that the first

representations of the new armaments in art date from about 400 BC.

Such was the new model army which Camillus created, and was to lead. He was consular tribune in 401 and 398 (traditional dates) and dictator in the vital year 396 (traditional date). The military problems were considerable. Veii was a fine natural site (see p. 114). At the end of the fifth century her natural defences were supplemented. The tufa cliffs were, where possible, cut back and elsewhere an earthen rampart with a stone breast-work was constructed to guard the weaker sections of the enceinte. The Roman armies must have aimed to seal Veii off from her allies. In this they were helped by the fact that there was very little national solidarity among the Etruscans. Veii's nearest neighbours, Capena and Falerii, may have helped, for they were harshly treated by Rome in the aftermath, but no one else seems to have become involved in the struggle. Caere, the Etruscan city of greatest resources close to Veii, seems, if anything, to have supported the Roman initiative (see p. 154). Nevertheless, the objective which the Romans had set themselves was a formidable one. Ancient technology favoured the defenders rather than the attackers. The Romans occupied the one neck of land that gave level access to the city from the north; but they were themselves vulnerable to attack from outside, and had little scope for manoeuvre against the city's defences.

It must have been a long and anxious fight. One army was tied down at Veii, but the danger from the Volscians and others to the south remained as persistent and aggravating as ever.

One significant episode concerned the key town of Satricum, which commanded one of the main corridors of South Latium. In the very year that Veii fell, the Romans dedicated a temple to Mater Matuta who was the principal goddess of Satricum and whose name is strongly Volscian in character. The archaeological evidence suggests that there may have been a joint shrine to Mater Matuta and Fortuna on the site of the temple at Rome from about 470 BC; but the main constructional work certainly belongs to the early fourth century. The goddess had a popular cult at Satricum, where a large quantity of votive offerings have been found dating, chiefly, from 420-

*c.*390 BC. The Roman temple, accompanied by a contemporary colony at Circeii near Satricum (Livy 5.24.4), points to
a combined military and religious policy to win over a dangerous area. The combination of force and religion is suggestive of Camillus. Nor did the internal situation show much
improvement. A severe plague in 399 (traditional date) led
to recourse to the Sibylline Books which recommended an
entirely strange innovation – a religious holiday during which
the images of the gods were set out on coaches and invited
to take part in a sacrificial feast (*lectisternium*). On this
occasion six deities were so honoured (Livy 5.13.6; Dionysius
12.9) – Apollo and Latona, powers of healing; Hercules and
Diana, as either agricultural powers, or patrons of men and
women; Mercury and Neptune, gods of trade and sea-faring.
The emergency must have been critical to have led to such
a startling novelty, and it may be that Camillus was, at least
in part, behind it. His was a religious upbringing and Livy
at least singles him out, like Aeneas, for his piety. This may
be no more than literary or artistic colouring, to give co-
herence to the character-drawing, but there are other indications that Camillus was a man of powerful religious feeling.
Some substance may also be given to this belief by the
probability that the ceremony was derived, not first hand
from Greece, but from Caere, the Etruscan city, with which
Camillus had close connections, as the events of the Celtic
invasion were to show (see p. 163). There are Etruscan pic-
tures which show comparable ceremonies.

Various tales are associated with the years that preceded
the eventual Roman success. Many of them are purely *post
eventum* fictions, but one thread runs through them all :
the tunnel. A Veientane prophet is captured and says that
until the level of the Alban Lake is controlled by a tunnel,
the Romans will not be able to capture Veii. The Romans
consult the Delphic oracle and receive substantially the same
reply. These stories are pure myth. The Alban Lake is many
miles away from Veii and not even in Etruria. Roman religious law forbade the consultation of foreign oracles, and
this embassy grew out of the fact that the Romans did make
a dedication at Delphi after the fall of Veii (see p. 157).
Nothing that occurred to the Alban Lake could have affected

Veii. The myths merely reinforce the tunnel theme. Now the Etruscans were master engineers. They constructed a fantastic number of underground drains to control the irrigation of their own countryside and Veii is no exception. Several drainage tunnels (*cuniculi*) in fact pass underneath the lines that separated the Roman blockading force from the main city and the traditional story is that the Romans gained access to the city by precisely such a tunnel. 'Camillus stopped pointless skirmishes that had occurred and directed his troops' minds to tunnelling. The soldiers were diverted to digging. Of these digging operations by far the most important and laborious was the construction of a tunnel to lead up into the central fortress; this work was now begun and to keep it going regularly the men were divided into six parties, working six hours each in rotation – as continuous labour underground would have exhausted them. The orders were that digging should go on day and night until the tunnel was complete' (Livy 5.19.9-11). What is to be made of this story? The tunnel probably existed already as part of the elaborate Veientane drainage system but was, in fact, utilized by the Romans to obtain entry into Veii. Some *cuniculi* appear to have been deliberately blocked with stones by the Veientanes to counter precisely this danger.

We may, therefore, accept the strength of the oral tradition that a tunnel played a decisive part in the fall of Veii.

Rome broke new ground after she had secured its surrender, and here again we may trace the hand of Camillus. In the past the Romans had been content to accept indemnities or to make alliances or treaties. On this occasion, however, they depopulated Veii and razed her defences. The destruction was not quite as complete as Roman authors liked, sentimentally, to portray. The scene of cattle grazing where once a great city had stood is contradicted by the archaeological evidence that some habitation continued and by the maintenance of a principal road through the site. Nevertheless it is substantially true. Veii ceased to exist as a major power and Roman settlers took over much of her land. It was distributed in parcels of three and a half acres – Livy says (5.30.7) to any free-born plebeian who wanted. The total number of recipients is not known but must have been considerable since it involved the creation of a new tribe, the Tromentina, to contain them, and gave rise to later legends that the Romans intended to migrate *en masse* to Veii. Some clue to the transformation is provided from the actual farms themselves. There was a change-over on Veientane sites from typically Etruscan Bucchero ware to a black-glazed ware about 410-390 BC. Out of approximately 100 sites from the area that have been investigated, one third have disclosed no black-glazed ware, that is they ceased to be occupied about 410-390 BC, i.e. as a result of the fall of Veii and the resettlement of the land by the Romans. The spread of black-glazed material on to other sites, however, indicates the distribution of new tenants or, at the very least, old tenants under new masters.

The decision was clearly a matter of major policy, and one which also involved a religious act, namely to transfer the allegiance of Veii's patron deity to Rome. It is true that Camillus' actions have been coloured by the later example of Scipio Aemilianus praying over the destruction of Carthage and enticing away her tutelary goddess to Rome; but there is no doubt that Veii's goddess became established at Rome, as Juno Regina, in 392 (traditional date) in a temple on the Aventine Hill near the medieval church of S. Sabina. Livy preserves the formula by which Camillus 'evoked' her (5.21.2): 'Queen Juno, to you I pray that you may leave this town where now you dwell and follow our victorious arms into our City of Rome, your future home, which will receive you in a temple worthy of your greatness.' The formula, which is no doubt an antiquarian's fabrication, is very like that used at Carthage in 146 BC by Scipio, which is preserved in the fifth-century scholar Macrobius (3.9.6): 'Whether it be a god or goddess in whose care is the people and city of Carthage, I implore and supplicate you who have the charge of this people and city and ask your pardon, that you should abandon the people and city of Carthage, and leave their sacred places, temples and city and depart from them, and that you should shed terror, fear and forgetfulness on that people and come propitiously to war and to my people at Rome, and that our sacred places, temples and city should be more acceptable to you and that you should be favourable towards me and the people of Rome and to my soldiers.' There is only one comparable parallel for such a major religious move, and that is the attempt to win over Castor and Pollux from the Latins in the 490s (see p. 99).

The capture of Veii, therefore, entailed great innovations both of a political and of a religious kind, and it was followed up by the subjugation of Veii's immediate allies, Capena and Falerii. The same aura of a religious crusade surrounds three other events which belong to this fateful episode of Roman history and which give support to the picture of Camillus as a man of dedicated vision. The first is a story that a golden bowl, which the Romans were sending to Delphi to dedicate as a thank-offering, was intercepted by some pirates from Lipari but released on the orders of the current chief magistrate of Lipari, Timasitheus. The truth of the story is confirmed by the fact that when the Lipari were annexed in 252 BC the descendants of Timasitheus were treated with scrupulous regard (Diodorus Siculus 14.93), and by explicit statements that, even after the bowl itself had been melted down by sacrilegious hands, the base survived in the treasury of the people of Marseilles at Delphi, for all to see down to the second century AD (Appian, *Ital.* 8). A religious gesture of a novel kind points once more to Camillus, especially in view of the circumstance that only Caere, of the cities close to Rome, is known to have had intimate links with Delphi, and Camillus, for his part, is known to have been in touch with Caere. Secondly, Camillus' sense of divine mission is reflected in the story, again probably influenced by Scipionic parallels, that he prayed, after the fall of Veii, that his success and the success of Rome should not seem excessive in the sight of heaven. In the event, despite his magnificent achievement in capturing Veii and uniting Rome under a common religious and military banner, Camillus was forced to leave the city two years later. The true reason cannot be recovered. The sources speak of popular jealousy at the mean way in which he distributed the booty. General suspicion of his intransigently purposeful politics may be more likely.

The third incident is even more questionable. On the news of his success at Veii unprecedented honours, it is said, were paid to Camillus. In particular he entered Rome in a triumphal chariot drawn by four white horses, a privilege

reserved for the gods, Jupiter and Sol. He also painted his
face with the red dye which customarily decorated the statues
of Jupiter (Pliny, *Natural History* 33.111). In other words,
Camillus is portrayed as having aspired to divinity. Now it
is certain that this tradition is false. The first historical figure
to have used such a divine four-horse chariot was Dionysius
I of Syracuse in 405 BC (Livy 24.5.4), and it is inconceivable
that the fashion could have spread so quickly to Rome, even
if the evidence did not in any case point to the influence of
the mystique of Alexander the Great as a major force in the
development of the triumph (see p. 39). When the tradition
was invented is not clear. It was certainly in the air at the
time that Caesar in 46 BC celebrated his triumph in comparable splendour. But it was either invented before that date
(and used by Caesar as a precedent) or soon after by his
friends – or enemies. For the Camillus story goes on to allege
that the outrage and unpopularity which his ostentation
aroused was the cause of his being exiled (Dionysius 52.13.3).
We simply do not know what actually happened to Camillus,
but it is perhaps significant that the legend which grew round
his name was one that hinged on his religious preoccupation.

Camillus is one of the few early Romans whose personality
we can attempt to appreciate across the centuries, even when
all allowance is made for the habit of Roman historians to
recast earlier figures in the guise of contemporary heroes –
Scipio, Sulla, Caesar, or even Augustus. One has only to assess
the military reforms which undoubtedly were made during
those decades, the military successes which attended Roman
arms during this period, the international initiative which cast
Rome for the first time in the role of an overtly imperialistic
and annexing power, and the religious devotion which inspired
and motivated these policies, to feel the driving force of a
statesman at work. The political dissensions are over-shadowed
by the force of a great man, but, as so often, the Romans
found it difficult to acclimatize themselves to such a personal
solution of their problems. Camillus might have shared the
fate of Julius Caesar: as it was, he temporarily had to abandon the political scene, just at the moment when his policies
had reaped complete success and when his vision and energy
were more urgently needed than ever before.

Roman history has so far been a parochial matter. The horizons of Roman statesmen were limited to her immediate surroundings – Latium and Southern Etruria, with the enemies who threatened her borders, the Aequi and the Volscians, the Sabines and the Etruscans. Only occasionally was she involved further afield : with Carthage at the height of regal prosperity (see p. 82), with Cumae, her nearest Greek neighbour, with Clusium and other Etruscan capitals, and rarely, indeed only when the corn-shortage was desperate, with Sicily. But now Rome became a cock-pit, which drew international armies to the fight, and as a result Rome became a topic of news-interest to contemporary Greek historians.

There were at least three forces on the move in the early fourth century which ultimately converged on Rome and caused the explosion.

The first of them was a movement of Celtic tribes from Gaul into the Po Valley (what was later known by the Romans as Cisalpine Gaul). Polybius says that the Celts came over the Eastern Alps from the Danube Basin about 400 BC.

It is not easy to plot these migrations. Livy, and other historians, give a different account.

A wave of Cenomanni, from Gaul, settled near where the towns of Brixia and Verona are today. After them came the Libui, the Salluvii who settled on the Ticinus, then the Boii and Lingones came over by the Poenine pass and finding all the country between the Alps and the Po already occupied, crossed the river on rafts and expelled the Etruscans. Finally [i.e. about 400 BC] the Senones, the last tribe to migrate, occupied all the country from the river Utens to the river Aesis. It was the Senones who attacked first Clusium and then Rome. (5.35.1-3)

Some control on this (obviously traditional) account can be obtained from archaeology; but a major difficulty arises from the fact that many of the Celts simply absorbed the culture of the communities where they settled, so that distinctive Celtic features immediately disappeared. Also much of the infiltration was slow and piece-meal : little groups settled for a while and then moved on. For the Celts were never city-builders. They preferred small villages (*oppida*) which afforded a temporary housing for a self-contained tribal unit. Nevertheless, Livy's account can be confirmed in outline and is to be preferred to the more clear-cut version of Polybius. The Po valley had been colonized by the Etruscans in the course of the fifth century, who founded towns at Milan (Melpum), Bologna (Felsina), Marzabotto, Mantua, Parma, Mutina, Piacenza and other key sites as well as the great cosmopolitan and commercial harbours on the Adriatic – Spina and Atria. But at much the same time the Celts are seen to infiltrate the area. In the region of the Italian lakes a gradual mixing of Celtic and native art is evident before the fourth century. Graves there contain Celtic iron-swords, Celtic brooches and wagon burials which are characteristic of the Celts. At Casila Valsenio near Ravenna, an inhumation was accompanied not only by Celtic pottery but also by a Greek black-figure vase dating 480-470 BC. So too Celtic metal-work has been recovered from fifth-century graves at Marzabotto and Bologna. Some of this may, of course, represent not Celtic burials but merely the stray products of trade, but the over-all impression is one of slow but steady penetration throughout the fifth and fourth centuries.

The confrontation is illustrated by some carved slabs (*stelae*) from Felsina, dating from about 350 BC, which prove continued and successful resistance (Plate 12). On these we see the horsemen of Felsina matched against naked Gauls : that the Etruscan is depicted as the victor, although the stone commemorates his death, need occasion no surprise! In effect the Gauls overran the whole Po Valley and the Etruscans were forced to disperse. Some fled to Piedmont and the surrounding areas : Etruscan inscriptions have been found there and in the hinterland of Nice. Others went north into the valleys of the Central Alps (Raetia) where they passed something of their alphabet and perhaps their language on to the natives who preserved it down to Livy's day. An anonymous geographer ('Scylax') writing about 375 BC gives a picture of the Adriatic coast, where the Etruscans only retained a small strip of coast around Spina while the Celts held the rest of the seaboard between Spina and the region of Venice.

The original cause of the Celtic migration is obscure. There was indeed a traditional explanation which Livy gives as follows (5.34):

> Tradition holds that Gauls were captivated by the attractions of the crops and especially by the novel pleasures of wine and, as a result, crossed the Alps and occupied lands previously cultivated by the Etruscans. Arruns of Clusium was responsible for introducing wine to the Gauls in order to entice the tribes over into Italy. He was annoyed that his wife had been seduced by a powerful young man to whom he had been tutor and from whom he could exact no revenge without outside help.

The story, reported also by Dionysius of Halicarnassus, is an old one. It was already known to Cato who alludes to it in the Second Book of his *Origins*, and it was told by a Greek playwright, Aristides of Miletus. But, although Professor Heurgon and others have claimed that it derives from Etruscan histories, there is no evidence that the Etruscans ever wrote history (see p. 15), and the story itself is a common folk-tale which recurs in several Greek migration legends. We simply do not know what impelled the Celts to move. There are no signs of the land-shortage or starvation which impelled some of the Greek colonists. It may have been no more than a matter of agricultural habit. As Caesar observed three hundred and fifty years later, the Celtic practice was to grow a year's crops and to graze a year's pasture and then to pass on to a fresh region. The community was always, therefore, on the move. Another attraction may have been the rich resources of iron-ore and other metals on Elba and in Northern Etruria, for the Celts were skilled and artistic metal-workers.

The Celts did settle some of the land that they overran, and they occupied it for hundreds of years until the Romans in their turn annexed Cisalpine Gaul, but they were essentially a nomadic people. They evolved sophisticated vehicles, two- and four-wheel carriages, in which they transported their belongings and which they, like the Boers, used as a mobile encampment. Such carriages, which are regularly depicted on Celtic monuments, account for the speed of travel which made the Celts famous. They were also a powerful fighting army. The Romans borrowed these inventions from them and most of the words which the Romans ordinarily used for carriages (*carpentum, essedum, rheda*, etc.) were also borrowed from the Celts. So, while some tribes settled quietly in the Po Valley and have left their mark both archaeologically and in the place-names ending in *-ago* which survive to this day (e.g. Ombriago, Maluago, Vercurago etc., near Bergamo), others moved restlessly onwards. Marzabotto was captured but only briefly held. There is a small Celtic cemetery, where iron-swords and other grave-goods have been found, and a concentration of small Celtic huts in the north part of the Etruscan city, but the evidence points to a short-lived occupation.

While this aimless activity was taking place in the north of Italy, there were other powers on the move in the South. Syracuse had for 100 years been the leading city of Sicily. In the early part of the fifth century great tyrants, such as Hiero, had made it a metropolis which won the principal contests at the Olympic Games and attracted the services of the most brilliant poets of Greece like Aeschylus and Pindar. The tyranny was superseded but more recently Syracuse had triumphantly defeated the might of two Athenian expeditions (415-412 BC) and had established itself as a military power to be respected. In 405 a young man of talent, Dionysius, was elected sole general and effectively re-established the tyranny. Dionysius had wide ambitions. He aimed to extend Syracusan control over the whole of Sicily and much of southern Italy as well as to humiliate the Carthaginians who still retained a foothold in Sicily (at Motya and elsewhere). In 392 BC he concluded a treaty with the Carthaginians which confined them to the north-west corner of the island, and which freed him to turn his attention to the mainland of Italy. For four years he campaigned until he succeeded in capturing Rhegium, the key city that opened the way to the north.

Greek, Carthaginian, Etruscan, Gaul: these were the four powers competing for the heart of Italy. The Carthaginians and the Etruscans were allies of long standing (see p. 82), but there was little that the Carthaginians could do to help. For the Etruscans, on the other hand, the threat was on two fronts. There is little sign that they made any concerted effort to unite in the face of the common danger, any more than they joined forces to go to the defence of Veii.

The only outward sign of preparation is the fact that the defensive walls of many Etruscan cities were constructed now – many of them formidable in size. The perimeter at Tarquinii is six miles long, at Volterra and Volsinii about five miles. But two cities at least, aware perhaps of her strategic position and her recently-demonstrated military power, made overtures to Rome. The first was Clusium which stood in the way of the Celtic advance. Clusium had long connections with Rome (see p. 88) and no doubt depended on Rome for salt and other Tiber-Valley trade. Livy says that she appealed to the Romans for help, who sent a delegation of Fabii, the usual Etruscan experts (see p. 115), to remonstrate with the Gauls. Their intervention served only to exacerbate matters. More probably, as Diodorus records, the Romans only went to reconnoitre what was happening. We hear of Roman military forces at Volsinii (Bolsena or Orvieto) and an unknown place nearby, Sapienum or Sappinum, in 388 BC. These are so far from Rome – at least sixty miles – that any thought of an aggressive expedition by the Romans is out of the question. The operations were either part of a general reconnaissance or part of an attempt to persuade the cities to make common cause against the invaders. In the event we hear nothing more of Clusium.

Caere, however, was much more intimately involved with Rome. From early times there may have been direct links. There is a tomb of the Tarquin family at Caere, in which no less than thirty-five members are recorded, and traditionally the royal Tarquins' first port of call after their exile was Caere (Livy 1.60.2). Throughout the fifth century Caere and Rome seem to have been at peace, if not in alliance. And indeed their interests were reciprocal. Caere had the only convenient ports for Rome to use, Pyrgi, Alsium (Palo) and Punicum (Santa Marinella) – since Ostia was still no more than a salt-working. Both Caere and Rome were cut off from the centre of Italy by Veii's sphere of influence, so that their inland trade was at the mercy of Veii. Both Caere and Rome appear to have reached specific understandings with the Carthaginians (see p. 83). Further signs of their cooperation may be inferred from two religious events associated with the war against Veii. Both of them – the first *lectisternium* at Rome and the prophecy about the Alban lake (see p. 154) – presuppose communications with Delphi, and Caere, we know, was the only Etruscan city that maintained a treasury at Delphi. It was natural that Rome's contact with Delphi should have been through the Caeretans.

It is this association between Rome and Caere which may provide the key to a major historical problem. Why did the Celts bother to attack Rome at all? True, she was beginning to make a name for herself but she was not worth a prolonged siege, and there were far more inviting targets. Four facts need to be taken together.

1. Shortly after the Celts had sacked Rome, they joined forces with Dionysius I (Justin 20.5.4-6).

2. The geographer Strabo, a contemporary of Livy who used much earlier sources, reports that when the Celts were leaving Rome after their successful devastation of the city, they were defeated by the Caeretans (5.220). (The same fact may be preserved by Diodorus [14.117.7] who reports that the Celts were defeated by the 'Cerii' in the 'Trausian' plain, but 'Trausian' is unidentifiable.)

3. Two years later Dionysius captured Pyrgi, Caere's port, as the culmination of two years' naval activity on the western coast of Italy (Diodorus 15.14.3-4).

4. The union of Caere and Rome during the Celtic invasions (see p. 170).

Collusion between Dionysius and the Gauls seems the obvious answer. Rome, as Caere's ally, was to be eliminated as part of an over-all plan for Dionysius to secure most of central Italy and Etruria with the help of Gallic pressure from the north.

Whatever the truth, Rome now emerged on to the world scene. This has one historical consequence of great importance. Hitherto we have been able to consider Rome's history in relative isolation. Only rarely has it impinged on international affairs. The Battle of Cumae (474 BC) is one of the few excep-

tions. For the most part Rome grew in a chrysalis, where
its own chronology and civilization, relative to its immediate neighbours, is all that matters to a historian. But with
the Celtic invasion Rome links up with a wider world and
we are able, for the first time, to fix Roman historical events
chronologically by the much more detailed and precise dates
of the Greek world. Aristotle knew of the Gallic capture
of Rome and this historical information was handed down
by Greek historians, so that Polybius, writing about 150
BC, could formulate an exact synchronism (1.6.1). 'Rome fell
to the Gauls nineteen years after the Battle of Aegospotami
[a naval battle in the war between Athens and Sparta], sixteen years before the Battle of Leuctra, and in the year when
the Peace of Antalcidas was signed [by the Greeks] with the
Persians and when Dionysius besieged Rhegium.' That is the
Christian year 387-6 BC. As has been explained (see p. 9)
the Romans had their own system of dating by annual magistracies, and their conventional dating was four years wrong,
since the equivalent Roman date was 390 BC, just as the
Roman date for the expulsion of the Tarquins was 510 BC
whereas the true date is, in all probability, 507 BC.

On 18 July 387 BC, a day whose memory was perpetuated
in the Roman calendar, the Roman army under Q. Sulpicius
was decisively beaten where the river Allia (Fosso della Bettina)
joins the Tiber a few miles up-stream from Rome. Apart from
the casualties in the battle itself, a number of Romans were
drowned trying to cross the Tiber, but the majority of sur-
vivors succeeded in making their way across the river to Veii.
Rome itself was largely undefended – indeed indefensible –
and lay open to the Gauls. Only the Capitol afforded any
stronghold.

The stories about the Gallic occupation are not in themselves significant; but they afford such an interesting example
of the way in which Roman history evolved that they are
well worth more detailed examination. The traditional account,
as given by Livy and Diodorus, can be briefly summarized.
When it was seen that there was no hope of saving Rome, the
Quirinal priest and the Vestal Virgins carried the sacred
treasures of Rome to safety at Caere. On their way they were
met by another refugee, L. Albinius, who transported them

on his cart. The remaining inhabitants retired to the Capitol apart from some elderly senators, who resolutely stayed at home and awaited death dressed in their official robes. The Gauls broke in and, provoked by the action of M. Papirius in striking one of them with his ivory baton as he stroked his beard, massacred them where they sat. The Gauls then fired large parts of the city. Meanwhile Roman hopes were pinned on Camillus who was living in exile at Ardea as a result of his fall from favour after the capture of Veii. Approaches were made to him to return and take over the command of the troops who had escaped the battle of the Allia to Veii. Camillus, however, demurred until he had received official approval from Rome itself. This was secured by the escapade of Pontius Cominius who floated down the Tiber, scaled the Capitol, secured the necessary authorization (a curiate law confirming Camillus' authority [*imperium*]: see p. 52) and returned the same way. Camillus then prepared to relieve Rome; but time was running out. A daring assault on the Capitol had only been prevented by the alarm raised by the sacred geese and the quick measures taken by M. Manlius. Hunger and disease were sapping both besiegers and besieged until a compromise was reached whereby the Gauls agreed to abandon Rome on the payment of a large indemnity. Just as the indemnity was being weighed out, Camillus arrived and broke up the negotiations. An immediate battle followed in the ruins of Rome and the Gauls were decisively beaten. So Camillus saved his city once again.

In attempting to unravel this skein, a modern historian has to try to distinguish those elements which were introduced in order to minimize Rome's actual humiliation, those elements which grew out of explanations of legal or religious practices, and those elements which were derived from corresponding Greek events, such as the sack of Athens by the Persians. What is left is likely to be the true residue of oral tradition.

1. Camillus' whole intervention and his defeat of the Gauls look very improbable. He is not mentioned at all by the historian Polybius. Even more significantly Aristotle, writing only fifty years after the events, mentions the saviour of Rome as 'Lucius'. Camillus' fore-name was 'Marcus' and 'Lucius' is probably L. Albinius who rescued the *sacra*. The

chief soldier was evidently Q. Sulpicius. So too the Roman victory is not known to historians before the second century and was invented to save Roman face on the model of the Caeretan victory mentioned by Strabo.

This leads one to wonder whether the legend that the Capitol held out is true either. The poet Ennius, writing soon after 200 BC, seems to imply that the Capitol as well as the rest of the city fell to the Gauls and this tradition is echoed 250 years later by another poet, Lucan. On the other hand there is no archaeological evidence (as there is for the rest of the city) of destruction, and the story of Manlius and the geese cannot be shaken. It has no Greek precursors and belongs to that very rare breed of indigenous Roman legends. The whole point of it is that the Gauls did *not* capture the Capitol. At least not then: perhaps they did later.

Camillus' eleventh-hour arrival as the indemnity was being weighed out can be cheerfully disregarded. That an indemnity was paid to persuade the Gauls to leave is, however, corroborated by the fact that some traders from Marseilles (one of the richest Greek colonies in the west which had long ties with Rome) contributed towards it, and the people of Marseilles were honoured by the Romans with special commercial privileges as a token of gratitude and recognition (Justin 43.5.10). But it raises two other problems. Traditionally it was 1,000 lbs. of gold, but in 52 BC Pompey, conducting excavations below the temple of Jupiter Optimus Maximus, found a cache of 2,000 lbs. There is, however, not the slightest reason to connect Pompey's find with the Gallic indemnity. Secondly, a proverb became associated with the indemnity. As the gold was being weighed out, the Romans complained that the weights were short measure; but the Gallic chief merely threw his sword on to the scales with the cry 'Hard luck on the conquered' (*vae victis*). This romantic scene serves merely to dramatize the old proverbial truth that justice (whose emblem is a sword) is always in the interest of the stronger.

2. The picturesque account of the massacre of the aged senators is clearly an anecdote that arose from a religious ritual whereby, in times of acute crisis, an ex-magistrate would solemnly vow himself to death for the sake of the whole people (*devotio*). A notorious case was that of P. Decius Mus

in 340 BC. The origin of the story is evident from the mention
of M. Papirius. The Papirii were a family who acted as a
repository of religious knowledge. The first *pontifex maximus*
and the first *rex sacrorum* of the new Republic in 507 BC
were allegedly Papirii and the earliest consolidate body of
religious law was known as the Ius Papirianum.

The exploit of Pontius Cominius belongs to a similar cate-
gory. There was a legal and religious issue. Could a man
assume command of a Roman army without having been properly invested with power? It was not just a matter of prac-
ticality. Unless he had full religious competence, he could not
consult the will of the gods before battle: indeed, he would
inevitably incur the displeasure of the gods, just as Crassus
did in 54 BC when he hurried off to the East without observing
the requisite ceremonies. So the Roman people and the Senate
had to be consulted. There may have been a family legend
among the Cominii that one of their number had slipped between the lines during the Gallic siege; but it has turned
into something very different.

One other minor episode is again an illustration of religious
demands. Many, if not all, Roman families had their own
family cults, often located in particular spots. To neglect
them was a serious breach of faith which would involve the
family in popular disgrace and divine displeasure. The elder
Cato once delivered a speech against a certain L. Veturius
justifying his action, as censor, in depriving him of his status
as a knight. One of Cato's complaints was that Veturius had
neglected his family cult which involved bringing water from
the river Anio to the shrine. During the Gallic siege, one of
the Fabii stationed on the Capitol, C. Fabius Dorsuo, slipped
through the lines to discharge the religious duties at their
family shrine on the Quirinal Hill. He was successful, but
his route was spotted and this inspired the Gauls to make an
attempt on the Capitol by the same path – an attempt which
only the geese frustrated. The story has probably no substance. It was invented to show the importance of family
cults and the piety of the Fabii in maintaining theirs.

So far what has emerged is that the Gauls besieged Rome
for several months and were heroically resisted by a garrison
on the Capitol, and that they were eventually bought off.

The only proof of it all lies in the ground. The main archaeological evidence comes from the Forum. A layer of broken
roof-tiles with carbonized wood and clay has been discovered
on the site of the Comitium (where the old Senate House had
stood), which can be dated to the early fourth century. Soon
afterwards, no doubt as part of the reconstruction, the whole
Forum was paved in *capellaccio*.

The final story to be considered is the removal of the sacred
treasures to Caere. These treasures (*sacra*) were stored in a
special room in the shrine of Vesta. Their precise identity is
uncertain. The scholar Varro said that they were seven
objects which guaranteed the safety of Rome (Servius, on
Aeneid 7.188): the needle of the mother of the gods, the terracotta chariot of Veii (see p. 84), the ashes of Orestes, the
sceptre of Priam, the veil of Ilione, the Palladium (a statue
of Pallas Athene said to have been brought from Troy) and
the shields of the Salii (*ancilia*). But his list probably dates
from the third century when Rome's pretensions to empire
were in the ascendant. The terracotta chariot could obviously
not be moved in any case. Besides there is another tradition
that two archaic jars (*doliola*) were part of the sacred treasures
and also two miniature statues of the Penates. Whatever
the treasures were, they represented the soul of Rome and
their survival assured Rome's survival. The action of L.
Albinius in helping to transport them to safety was regarded,
in the religious climate of the times, as of more importance
than any military engagement. This is why Aristotle refers
to him as the saviour of Rome. This is why a much later
statesman who married an Albinia called his son Quirinalis
to commemorate the part played by the *flamen Quirinalis* in
association with L. Albinius. And this is why a commemorative inscription was set up centuries later. It reads:

[When the Gauls were be]sieging the Capitol
he led the [Ve]stal [Virgins] to Caere:
There he made it his responsibility to ensure
that the [sacrifices] and ceremonial rituals were not
[interrup]ted.
[When the city was reco]vered he brought back
the sacred objects and the Virgins [to Rome].

The authenticity of Caere's safeguarding Rome's treasures is borne out by the appreciation that was shown to her subsequently. Unluckily this has become one of the most disputed issues in Roman history, because there is a serious conflict of evidence. Livy reports that the Caeretans were honoured with 'public hospitality', that is a special status which allowed them to come and go in Rome without being subject to any of the requisitions or taxes to which Roman citizens were liable (5.50.3). In later times, however, there was a register, known as the Caeretan Tables, which was compiled by the censors and contained the names of citizens who, for one reason or another, had been deprived of the vote (Aul. Gell. 16.13.7; Horace, *Epistles* 1.6.62-3). To be on this register was a mark of black disgrace: it meant that one was a citizen, with all the obligations, taxes, requisitions expected of a citizen, but without the franchise. There is here a clear contradiction, which has been explained in two main ways: 1. The status of a citizen without the franchise was originally an honourable and prized one which in course of time became devalued into a second-class citizenship. It was this honour which the Caeretans were accorded in 386 BC but which Livy has mistakenly identified with a different grant of 'public hospitality'. 2. The Caeretans were indeed granted 'public hospitality' in 386 BC but the relations between Rome and Caere deteriorated over the next hundred years until a situation was reached (Toynbee suggests in 274-3 BC) when Caere was virtually annexed as an inferior community with vote-less citizenship. The second explanation seems the one to fit the nature and the history of the relationship between the two cities much more satisfactorily.

When the dust had settled and the Gauls had packed their tents, when the *sacra* had returned home from Caere and the fighting between Etruscans, Gauls and Sicilians had petered out, where did Rome stand? It is not easy to recover the truth. Ancient and modern historians tend to think of Rome's advance to world power as a straightforward progression. In fact, however, the years after 386 BC mark the end of an epoch. The city itself was a shambles. Much rebuilding had to be done, and was done, as after the Great Fire of London, on a makeshift basis, as the alignment of the streets reveals.

Externally, Rome still retained control of the Veientane territory, although a persistent rumour that the Roman people
wanted to migrate to Veii from the debris of their own city,
together with the fact that the remnants of the Roman army
had regrouped there after the Allia, might be taken to mean
that for a time Veii recovered some of her independence.
Elsewhere, however, the situation was black. The Latin League
was left without Roman support and various joint colonies –
Velitrae, Vitellia, Satricum – disappear from sight and are
absorbed by a confident and resurgent Volscian nation. In
effect the Latin League is dissolved and the frontiers of
Rome in Latium revert to what they had been a hundred
years before. Internally there was no time for politics. Camillus and Manlius led a popular revival, but the great political
problems remained in abeyance until Rome could once again
afford the luxury of party-warfare. Very little had changed
since the time of the Decemvirate, two generations before.

The Gallic Sack marks one of the great moments of Roman
history. It closes a particular stage of historical evolution.
By Roman chronology it fell in the 365th year of the city
– a Great Year, since there are 365 days in a year, as Livy
makes Camillus remind his audience (5.54.5), just as 365 years
after the Crucifixion, in AD 398, men were also seriously
apprehensive that an age was drawing to a close.

Date Chart

The dates here given are the conventional dates which for much of the Monarchy are almost entirely notional (and are, therefore, noted as *trad.*) and which for the Republic are likely to be three or four years too early (e.g. the capture of Rome by the Gauls is synchronized by the earliest authorities with Greek events securely dated to 386 BC but the conventional Roman chronology dated it to 390 BC).

	Roman Events		*External Events*
		856	(trad.) Foundation of Carthage
753	(trad.) Foundation of Rome		
625–600	Arrival of Etruscans at Rome		
616–578	(trad.) L. Tarquinius Priscus	594	Archonship of Solon at Athens
578–534	(trad.) Servius Tullius	c.547	Battle of Alalia
c.540	Temple of Diana		
534–510	(trad.) L. Tarquinius Superbus	510	Expulsion of Pisistratids
510	Expulsion of Tarquins Temple of Jupiter Optimus Maximus Treaty with Carthage		
507–6	Attack by Porsenna on Rome		
? 506	Battle of Aricia		
497	Temple of Saturn		
466	Battle of Lake Regillus		
496–5	Latin Treaty of Sp. Cassius		
495	Temple of Mercury		
494	First Secession of the Plebs		

	Roman Events		External Events
493	Temple of Ceres	490	Battle of Marathon
486	Coup of Sp. Cassius		
479	Battle of Cremera	479	Battle of Thermopylae
		474	Battle of Cumae
471	Creation of tribal assembly	470	Penetration of Italy by Celts
451	Decemvirate		
449	Second Secession of the Plebs	449	Peace of Callias
	Consulship of Valerius and Horatius		
444	Institution of Military Tribunes	443	Foundation of Thurii
443	Institution of Censorship		
441	Coup of Sp. Maelius	431–404	War between Athens and Sparta
c.437–26	War with Fidenae		
		429	Plague at Athens
		423	Capture of Capua by Oscans
		421–0	Capture of Cumae by Oscans
		405	Battle of Aegospotami
406–396	War with Veii	405–367	Dionysius I, Tyrant of Syracuse
396	Capture of Veii		
390	Capture of Rome by Gauls	386	Peace of Antalcidas

Primary Sources

VARRO M. Terentius Varro (116 BC–27 BC.). Roman anti-quarian who wrote extensively on Roman customs, rites and traditions. His *Antiquities* does not survive but was widely quoted by later writers. He was called 'the most learned of the Romans'. His surviving works on the *Latin Language* and *Agriculture* are published in the Loeb Classical Library, with translation.

CICERO M. Tullius Cicero (106 BC–43 BC). Although primarily an advocate and politician, he was deeply interested in history and knowledgeable about it. His fragmentary work *On the Republic* contains valuable information; there is an annotated translation by G. H. Sabine and S. B. Smith in the Library of Liberal Arts, under the title *On the Commonwealth*.

DIONYSIUS Born in Halicarnassus, Asia Minor, he went to Rome in 30 BC where he lived until his death in 8 BC. He wrote *Roman Antiquities*, a history of Rome to 264 BC in Greek, which incorporates much evidence from earlier writers: also rhetorical works. Text in the Loeb Classical Library, with translation.

STRABO (Aelius) Strabo, Greek geographer and historian who settled in Rome in 29 BC. His *Geography* contains interesting foundation legends and other details. Text in the Loeb Classical Library, with translation.

VIRGIL P. Vergilius Maro, of Mantua (70 BC–19 BC). Roman poet whose works, especially the *Aeneid*, incorporate many legends and traditions of early Rome. There is a prose translation of the *Aeneid* in Penguin Classics; the poetic version by C. Day Lewis is also good.

LIVY   T. Livius, of Padua (59 BC–AD 17). He wrote the history of Rome from the foundation to 9 BC in 142 books, of which 1–10, and 21–45 survive. His primary interests were artistic and philosophical; but his work contains a great deal of original material and is the most important single source for the period. Full text in the Loeb Classical Library, with translation; commentary by R. M. Ogilvie on Books 1-5, Clarendon Press, 1969; translation of Books 1-5 in Penguin Classics under the title *The Early History of Rome.*

OVID   P. Ovidius Naso (43 BC–AD 18). A Roman poet, some of whose works, especially the *Fasti* – a poetical account of the Roman calendar – contain precious details of early religious rites. Text in the Loeb Classical Library, with translation.

PLUTARCH   Q. Mestrius Plutarchus, Greek historian and philosopher, from Chaeronea in Boeotia (*c.* AD 45–*c.*120). Widely travelled scholar who acquired Roman citizenship and was deeply interested in Roman history. In addition to antiquarian works, he wrote a series of parallel Greek and Roman lives, including Romulus, Numa, Publicola, and Camillus, which contain much original research on early Rome. Text in the Loeb Classical Library, with translation.

FESTUS   Sex. Pompeius Festus (*fl.* AD 150). Author of a dictionary (an abridgement of an earlier one by Verrius Flaccus) which contains much antiquarian and religious information, associated with archaic words. Text in the Teubner series.

*

TIMAEUS   Greek historian from Taormina in Sicily (*c.* 350 BC–260 BC). The first Greek historian to write extensively about Italian and Roman history. His work survives only in quotations, to be found in Jacoby, *Fragmente der Griechischen Historiker*, no. 566.

FABIUS

Q. Fabius Pictor, the first Roman historian (*fl.* 225–200 BC). His work survives only in summaries and quotations but he was responsible for formulating much of the history of the Kingdom and early Republic. Fragments in Peter, *Historicorum Romanorum Reliquiae.*

PISO

L. Calpurnius Piso (consul 130 BC). The first Roman historian to make extensive use of archival material from early Rome. His work survives only in fragments and quotations, to be found in Peter, *Historicorum Romanorum Reliquiae.*.

Further Reading

1 Historical Introduction

The best general introduction to Italy and the Etruscans is
M. Pallotino's *The Etruscans* (Harmondsworth, 1955). A more technical study, with the most recent archaeological evidence, is
given by H. Hencken, *Tarquinia and Etruscan Origins* (London,
1968).

The archaeological evidence for early Rome itself is best found
in the series of volumes entitled *Early Rome* by the great Swedish
archaeologist Einar Gjerstad and published by the Swedish Institute at Rome (1953 – 1973); Vol. 6 contains his historical survey.
Roman chronology is still controversial. Gjerstad champions the
later dates, but other scholars, notably H. Müller-Karpe, in two
books *Von Anfang Roms* (Heidelberg, 1959) and *Zur Stadtwerdung
Roms* (Heidelberg, 1962) make a strong case for an earlier chronology. There is a good critique of the problem by D. Ridgway,
Journal of Roman Studies 58 (1968) pp. 235–40.

J. Heurgon's, *The Rise of Rome to 264 BC* (London, 1973) is a
wide-ranging study which sets Rome in its total Mediterranean
context.

2 Sources

The fragments of early Roman historians are collected by H.
Peter, *Historicorum Romanorum Reliquiae* (Leipzig, 1906). The
main surviving historians have not yet been fully edited, apart
from Livy, Books 1-5, Oxford, 1965; second edition, 1969).

Useful summaries of the reliability and tendentiousness of
early Roman historians will be found in P. G. Walsh *Livy: His
Historical Aims and Methods* (Cambridge, 1961) and E. Badian,
Latin Historians (ed. T. A. Dorey: London, 1966). There are also
sound accounts of Livy as a historian by Sir Ronald Syme,
Harvard Studies in Classical Philology, 65 (1954), pp. 27–88 and
J. Briscoe in *Livy* (ed. T. A. Dorey: London, 1971).

The written sources are very fully discussed – but with a
pronounced bias – by E. Gjerstad, *Early Rome* 5 (Lund, 1973).

3   The Arrival of the Etruscans

Gjerstad (p. 177) gives the best account of the archaeology of early
Rome. The facts about the Aeneas legend are well collected by
G. K. Galinsky, *Aeneas, Sicily and Rome* (Princeton, 1969). More
recently a seventh-century tomb, subsequently converted in the
fourth century BC into a shrine, has been identified with what
Dionysius of Halicarnassus knew as the shrine of Aeneas. (*Il
Messagero* 30 June 1972, P. Sommella, *Atti d. pontificio accademia
di Archeologia: Rediconti* 44, 1971-2, pp. 47-74, and *Gymnasium* 81,
1974, pp. 273-97.)   For Aeneas and Romulus see T. J. Cornell,
Proceedings of the Cambridge Philological Society 21 (1975), pp.
1-32.
     Roman religion is a fraught field. G. Dumézil's *Archaic Roman
Religion* (Eng. tr. London, 1970) is one of the most accessible
books but cannot be relied on. The most authoritative recent
study is in German: K. Latte, *Römische Religionsgeschichte*
(Munich, 1960). The older works by W. Warde-Fowler, *The Roman
Festivals* (London, 1908) and H. J. Rose, *Ancient Roman Religion*
(London, 1949) contain the basic evidence. F. Altheim's *History of
Roman Religion* (Eng. tr. by H. Mattingly: London, 1938) is highly
stimulating but explains the evidence too much in Greek terms.
     There is a very full account of the triumph by H. Versnel,
Triumphus (Leiden, 1970) which can be supplemented by the
ideas of S. Weinstock (*Divus Julius*, Oxford 1971) and L. Bon-
fante Warren in the *Journal of Roman Studies* 60 (1970), 49-66;
Studies in Honour of J. Alexander Kerns (The Hague, 1970). There
is a detailed history of the calendar by A. K. Michels, *The
Calendar of the Roman Republic* (Princeton, 1967).
     The weapons of early times are illustrated by R. Bloch, *The
Origins of Rome* (London, 1960). A. M. Snodgrass in the *Journal of
Hellenic Studies* 85 (1965), pp. 110-22 definitely establishes the
date for the adoption of hoplite armour in central Italy. The
early organization of the army is obscure. The facts are assembled
by R. E. A. Palmer, *The Archaic Community of the Romans* (Cambridge, 1970) but he explains the evidence almost exclusively in
terms of *curiae*. G. V. Sumner, in the *Journal of Roman Studies* 60
(1970), pp. 67–78, gives a coherent account of the development of
the army.
     The relative importance of the cavalry and its relationship with
the patrician order has been disputed by A. Alföldi in *Early Rome
and the Latins* (Ann Arbor, 1965) and A. Momigliano in the

Journal of Roman Studies 56 (1966), pp. 16-24. Subsequent articles in *Historia* have not affected the main issues.

4   The Making of One Nation

M. Lejeune is the leading authority on the Latin alphabet. He gives a clear statement of the position in the *Revue des Etudes Latines* 35 (1957), pp. 88 ff. On the internal organization of Rome R. E. A. Palmer (*The Archaic Community*) should be consulted for the evidence and for some stimulating speculations. Dumézil, a distinguished French scholar and anthropologist, has traced in a series of studies – especially *Jupiter, Mars, Quirinus* (Paris, 1949) – common patterns of belief and social organization among two European peoples, which, he claims, derive from their common ancestry. Professor L. R. Taylor gives a lucid traditional account of the tribal organization in *The Voting Districts of the Roman Republic* (Papers and Memoirs of the American Academy at Rome, XX, 1960).

The references to the controversy between Alföldi and Momigliano are given in the further reading for Chapter 3. The authenticity of the census figures is examined by A. J. Toynbee, *Hannibal's Legacy* (Oxford, 1965) 2, pp. 438-79; calculations of the acreage of land occupied by Rome at this time, when compared with analogous communities, suggest that the total male population may not have been more than 30,000.

Momigliano discusses the character of the patricians and the plebeians in a number of articles. The most accessible is 'The Origins of the Roman Republic', in *Interpretation: Theory and Practice*, (ed. C. S. Singleton: Baltimore, 1969), pp. 1–34.

5   Servius Tullius

The decisive contribution to the understanding of Servius Tullius' reforms remains the article by H. Last in the *Journal of Roman Studies* 35 (1945), pp. 30–48.

Momigliano (*Rend. Accad. Lincei* 17 [1962], pp. 387 ff.) and Alföldi (*Early Rome and the Latins*, pp. 47 ff.) offer divergent accounts of the cult of Diana on the Aventine.

6   *Tarquinius Superbus*

The best account of the temple of Jupiter Optimus Maximus is by E. Gjerstad, *Early Rome*, 4, pp. 588 ff. Versnel's discussion of the games will be found in his book *Triumphus*. There is a clear account of the expansion of Rome under the Tarquins in H. H. Scullard's *The Etruscan Cities and Rome* (London, 1967), especially pp. 243 ff. J. Heurgon gives an admirable description of Etruscan civilization in his *Daily Life of the Etruscans* (London, 1964).

7   *The Fall of the Monarchy*

All the main topics are treated by Alföldi in *Early Rome and the Latins*.

The date of the institution of the Republic is highly controversial. Among those who want to bring it down to the fifth century are R. Werner in *Der Beginn der Römischen Republik* (Munich, 1964), Gjerstad, especially in *Legends and Facts of Early Rome* 'Lund, 1962) and Bloch in *The Origin of Rome* and *Tite-Live et les premiers siècles de Rome* (Paris, 1965). There is a useful review of the arguments about the plebeian names in the Fasti by A. Drummond in the *Journal of Roman Studies* 60 (1970), pp. 199 ff. The Fasti are most conveniently consulted in T. S. R. Broughton, *Magistrates of the Roman Republic* (New York, 1951). The problems of the early Republic were the theme of a symposium organized by the Fondation Hardt. The papers and the discussion which followed were published in 1968. E. Pais (*Ancient Italy*, London, 1908) was one of the most astute critics at detecting Greek myths which have been transplanted to Rome.

The treaties between Carthage and Rome are highly controversial. The discussion by F. W. Walbank on the relevant chapter of Polybius in his *Historical Commentary on Polybius* (Oxford, 1957) is the best summary of opposing views. They are also discussed by A. J. Toynbee (*Hannibal's Legacy* pp. 519-555). On the Pyrgi inscription the most reliable account is probably that by J. Heurgon in the *Journal of Roman Studies* 56 (1966), pp. 1 ff. The excavations of the Regia have been conducted and published by Frank Brown (e.g. in *Les Origines de la République Romaine*, pp. 47–64).

J. Heurgon considers the office of *praetor maximus* in the same volume (pp. 99–132). E. S. Staveley, in an article reviewing the development of the Roman constitution (*Historia* 5, 1956, pp. 99 ff.) would date the law in question to 342 BC.

A vivid account of the François tomb will be found in J. Heurgon's *Daily Life*, pp. 45–9 but one should also read Momigliano, *Claudius* (Oxford, 1934), pp. 12 ff. (For the excavations at San Giovanale see the publications by the Swedish Institute at Rome.) On Aristodemus and his policy there are recent discussions by B. Combet Farnoux, *Mélanges d'Archéologie et d'Histoire* 69 (1957), pp. 7–44 and C. G. Hardie, *Papers of the British School at Rome* 37 (1969), pp. 17–19.

Momigliano's 'An Interim Report on the Origins of Rome' (*Journal of Roman Studies* 53 [1963], pp. 96 ff.) is fundamental reading for the whole period.

8 The Early Years of the Republic

A very thorough survey of the walls of Rome was written by G. Säflund (*Le Mura di Roma*, 1932). There has been little development since that work. The discoveries at Lavinium have not been fully published yet, but Alföldi gives a useful summary of what is known. On lake Regillus see *Hommages à M. Renard* (Brussels, 1969), 2, pp. 566 ff. Weinstock's discussion of the Aeneas inscription will be found in the *Journal of Roman Studies* 50 (1960), pp. 117 ff.; the Castor and Pollux inscription was published by F. Castagnoli in *Studi e Materiale* 30 (1959), pp. 109 ff. A. Drummond pursues the independent development of the Aeneas story at Rome and Lavinium in the *Journal of Roman Studies* 62 (1972), pp. 219.

The date and terms of the Latin treaty are the subject of a close investigation by Werner (see further reading for Chapter 7) who favours a date some thirty years later than that defended here, and also by Toynbee (*Hannibal's Legacy*, pp. 120 ff.). The analysis of imported pottery is derived from Gjerstad, *Early Rome* 4, pp. 593 ff. Momigliano was the first to stress the Hellenic orientation of the plebeians in founding the cult of Ceres (*Les Origines de la République Romaine*, pp. 216 ff.). The clearest account of *nexum* is that given by Professor M. I. Finley, *Revue d'Histoire du Droit* 43 (1965), pp. 159 ff.

9   The Decemvirate

Rome's relations with Etruria are covered not only by H. H. Scullard's book but also by W. V. Harris, *Rome in Etruria and Umbria* (Oxford, 1971), pp. 4-49. The archaeology of Veii and surrounding country has been studied by the British School of Rome since the early 1950s and the results are contained in a number of papers published in the series *Papers of the British School at Rome*.

The social background of the Twelve Tables is ably discussed by F. Wieacker (*Les Origines de la République Romaine*, pp. 295–356). The fragments of the laws themselves are collected in *Fontes Iuris Romani Anteiustiniani* (ed. S. Riccobono: Florence, 1941), and are studied in an important forthcoming book by Alan Watson. For the possible reform of the calendar see A. K. Michels (p. 178 above).

10   Political Reform after the Decemvirate

E. S. Staveley outlines his views on the Valerio-Horatian laws in *Historia* 3 (1955), pp. 427 ff.

My interpretation of the matrimonial issues at stake over the Maid of Ardea, first put forward in *Latomus* 21 (1962), 477-83, is restated to meet the criticism of Professor Daube, *Aspects of Roman Law* (Edinburgh, 1969), pp. 112–16.

The origin of the consular tribunate, and in particular whether it was inspired by military or political considerations, continues to be debated. Of recent contributions the most valuable are by F. E. Adcock, *Journal of Roman Studies* 47 (1957), pp. 9–14; A. Boddington, *Historia* 8 (1959), pp. 356–64; R. E. A. Palmer, *The Archaic Community of the Romans*, pp. 223–63; G. V. Sumner, *Journal of Roman Studies* 60 (1970), pp. 63-73; J. Pinsent, *Historia: Einzelschriften Heft* 24 (1975). The meaning of *lustrum condere* is analysed by me in the *Journal of Roman Studies* 51 (1961), pp. 31-9.

11   Military and Economic Difficulties 440–410

The history of Apollo at Rome has been written by J. Gagé (*L'Apollon Romain*, Paris, 1955), but some of his theories are unacceptable. On the custom of throwing 60-year-olds from the bridge see Palmer, *Archaic Community*, pp. 90. Livy's reference to Augustus and the corselet of Cossus is probably a later addition to his History, made about 25 BC, as is argued by T. J. Luce, *Transactions of the American Philological Association* 96 (1965), pp. 209 ff. The story of Sp. Maelius has been most recently examined by A. W. Lintott in *Violence in Republican Rome* (Oxford, 1963), pp. 55 ff., which is a good introduction both to the problems of lawlessness at Rome and to the way in which Roman legends evolved.

12. Veii

The Etruscan drainage system has been studied by S. Judson, *Papers of the British School at Rome* 31 (1963), pp. 67–92. The legends about Veii are imaginatively analysed in a book by J. Hubeaux, *Rome et Véies* (Paris, 1958). The archaeological discoveries for the land of Veii are catalogued by J. B. Ward-Perkins and others, *Papers of the British School at Rome* 36 (1968).

E. Rawson (*Papers of the British School at Rome* 39 [1971], pp. 13–31) makes a cautious reconstruction of the Roman military organization before the second century and tends to discount Camillus' contribution to reform.

On Camillus' triumph and exile see Momigliano, *Classical Quarterly* 36 (1942), pp. 111–20 and S. Weinstock *Divus Julius* (Oxford, 1972).

13 The Gallic Disaster

The Celtic invasion of the Po Valley has so far been only cursorily investigated. There is valuable material in E. Baumgaertel, *Journal of the Royal Anthropological Institute* 67 (1937), pp. 231-86 and a good résumé in L. Barfield, *Northern Italy* (London, 1971), pp. 146–59. The most recent analysis is by P. Tozzi, *Storia Padana Antica* (Milan, 1972) but the Celtic evidence is not well documented.

Early Rome and the Etruscans

M. Sordi (*I Rapporti Romano-Ceriti*, Rome, 1960) offered an extremely original and provocative estimate of the relations between Rome and Caere at this time. The technical question of the status of the Caeritans is discussed by W. V. Harris, *Rome in Etruria and Umbria* (Oxford) 1971, pp. 45–7 and Toynbee, *Hannibal's Legacy*, p. 411.

General Index

P. Accoleius Lariscolus, 67
L. Aelius Stilo Praeconinus, 120
Sex. Aelius Paetus, 119
Q. Aelius Tubero, 21
Mam. Aemilius, 142
Aeneas, 33-5, 98
Aequi, 89, 111
Aequimaelium, 144
Alalia, 82
Alban Lake, 154
L. Albinius, 109, 165
Algidus, 111, 146
Allia, 165
Alphabet, 49
Annales Maximi, 18
Ti. Antistius, 146
Antium, 76, 82, 95, 111
Ardea, 76, 82, 98, 103, 131, 139
Argei, 77, 138
Aricia, 67, 73
Aristides of Miletus, 161
Aristodemus, 89
Aristotle, 22, 165
Artemus, 65
A. Aternius, 119
Atria, 100
Aucno, 50
Augustus, 23-4, 141
Auspices, 57, 130, 133
Aventine Hill, 67, 69, 107-8, 156

Bologna, 11, 160
Bola(e), 139, 140

Caecilius of Calacte, 21
Caelian Hill, 88
Caere, 62, 65, 83, 153, 157, 163ff
Calendar, 40-2, 124
Camillus, see M. Furius Camillus
Campania, 13
C. Canulaius, 130
Capena, 113, 153, 157
Capitol, the, 167
Capua, 86
Carthage, 75, 82ff, 156, 159
Carventum, 139
Casa Romuli, 11
Casila Valsenio, 160
Sp. Cassius, 20, 100, 110, 123, 128
Cato, see M. Porcius Cato
Cavalry, 43ff, 152
Celeres, 44
Celts, 159
Censor, 134
Ceres, 42, 107, 117, 128
Cicero, see M. Tullius Cicero
Cincinnatus, see L. Quinctius Cincinnatus
Circeii, 75, 82, 94, 154
Circus Maximus, 32, 72
Classis, 45-6, 53, 133
Claudii, 59, 90-1
Claudius, Ap. the Decennis, 125
Claudius, the Emperor, 63, 87
Altus Clausus, 90
Clients, 60
Cloaca Maxima, 31
Tullus Cluilius, 143

Index to Sources